Fire in the Hole

THE SPIRIT WORK OF

FI YI YI &

The Neighborhood Story Project
An imprint of
the University of New Orleans Press

© 2018
All Rights Reserved
Printed in Lithuania

All photographs by Jeffrey David Ehrenreich
unless otherwise stated. © 2018 All Rights Reserved

Series Editor: Helen A. Regis
Graphic Designer: Gareth Breunlin
Photo Editor: Bruce Sunpie Barnes

Title page: Beadwork detail from Fi Yi Yi's Orange suit.
Left: Beadwork from the 2017 Fi Yi Yi shield.
Photographs by Jeffrey David Ehrenreich.

Opposite Page: Altar dedicated to Collins "Coach" Lewis created by Sylvester Francis, with a photograph by Christine Breault, on display at the Backstreet Cultural Museum.

NEIGHBORHOOD STORY PROJECT
Our Stories Told By Us
P.O. Box 19742
New Orleans, LA 70179
www.neighborhoodstoryproject.org

A POWERHOUSE OF KNOWLEDGE
1116 Henriette Delille Street
New Orleans, LA 70116

Fire in the Hole was made possible by generous support from
the University of New Orleans, the Surdna Foundation,
the New Orleans Jazz & Heritage Foundation, the Arts Council
of New Orleans, the Louisiana Division of the Arts, the
City of New Orleans, and funds raised by our community during
UNO Press & the Neighborhood Story Project's annual Write-A-Thon.

Printed by KOPA® www.kopa.eu

Dedication

To Collins "Coach" Lewis.

We had a journey like nobody else.

You made everything possible.

And we'd always begin with you saying,

"I'm telling you, don't get me started…"

The co-director of the Backstreet Cultural Museum, Domonique Dilling, holds a picture of her great-grandmother, Big Queen Anita, masking with the Eighth Ward Hunters. The photograph is on display at the Backstreet. Anita was also the grandmother of Christine Harris, Victor Harris's wife. Photograph by Bruce Sunpie Barnes.

Acknowledgments
Many hands and hearts went into making this book possible.

From Victor Harris

Above all, I thank God.

To our ancestors who went before us.

To all my family members for their support. My parents, brothers and sisters, nieces and nephews are all a part of the tribe. When my mother passed away, she had 213 grandchildren and great-grandchildren.

To Martha Sims and our children Tinika, Angela, and Victor Jr., who were with me when the Spirit of Fi Yi Yi started out.

To Judy Hunter and our child, Adrian.

To my beautiful wife, Christine Harris, and our children Clarence, Curtis, and Dijonaise.

To my closest friend, Lawrence "Chicken" Journey.

To the Yellow Pocahontas and the memory of Allison "Tootie" Montana. To Jerome Smith for pulling Yellow Pocahontas together with Tambourine & Fan and strengthening our community.

To the coaches of Hunter's Field: Alvin Landry, Winston Landry, Sam Griffin, William Harris, Joe Lindsey, Collins "Coach" Lewis, and Big Ike Bennett. I also want to mention Frank "Captain Kicks" Mitchell who was with us all the time. You were the foundation, the soldiers, and the workers. You did it all.

To Matthew Boutte and the other children we have lost to violence. We won't forget.

To the neighbors of my community where the Spirit of Fi Yi Yi was born.

To all the people who helped sew at the table: Alton Quinn, Darryl Lewis, Curt Lewis, Brian "Eddie Pint" Harris, Clifford Harris, Groovy Gus, Edward Emery, Margie, Jill, Samuel Graham, Alvin Landry, Winston Landry, Milton Smith, Sam Griffin, William Harris, Joe Lindsey, Collins "Coach" Lewis, Big Ike Bennett, and Fred "Redhead" Williams.

To everyone who masked with Fi Yi Yi and to all those who have followed me over the years.

To Sylvester Francis of the Backstreet Cultural Museum for being our caretaker and supporter for so many years, and for making this book with us.

To all the friends who have shared their documentary work with us over the years, including Cynthia Becker, Christine Breault, Freddye Hill, George Ingmire, Lisa Katzman, Claire Tancons, Aaron Walker, Eric Waters, and Yuki Yamaguchi.

To all the tribes who participate in the culture.

And last, but not least, to the city of New Orleans. There's no place like home.

From Jack Robertson

To my mother and father, Laura and Wilbert Roberton, for staying with me and pushing me to do right and not get in trouble. They always told me that I would be something; I just needed to try harder.

To my son, Justin, his wife Tiffany, and my grandchildren: Jada, Ms. Robinson, Mimi, and Muffie. My grandkids ask me, "Where are you going?" I tell them, "Everybody love Jack. I stay busy." They say, "Well, Papa, everybody love you here, too."

To my chief and Coach, who always told me I was blessed to have the talent that I have.

To all the ones who are not here, I appreciate what I learned from you. I miss all the people who were part of the tribe when I first joined. Sam Griffin showed me how to do wire work. I want to give special thanks to him. I hope we have a few more years of happiness like we had back then.

And to our only Jewish Indian, Jeffrey. I love you, too. I love everyone.

From Wesley Phillips

A thank you goes out to all who have contributed to my 25 years as a drummer with the Mandingo Warriors.

My family: To my mother, Helen Robinson Phillips, for all the love and support she gave to me and my many musical endeavors. To my brothers, Edward Joseph, Earl Phillips, and Byron Phillips, for their help and assistance when I returned to the Seventh Ward. To my daughters Tiombe and Ebony Phillips who traveled with me to several African drum and dance conferences. To my nephew, Edward Jackson, for the many years of drumming together, including several years as a drum section member.

Ninth Ward Funk: To the Energy Funk Band, SUNO Drum Ensemble, Desire Poets, and the Desire Community Choir who were with me during my early developmental years playing with drummers, singers, and musicians. To the many residents of the Desire Projects who would sing while beating out rhythms in the hallways.

The Mardi Gras Sound: All the singers, drummers, and tambourine players I heard at the Indian practices, Super Sundays, Mardi Gras Indian Hall of Fame events, funerals, and festivals held throughout the city.

The Keepers of African Rhythms: To Stephen Kenyatta Simon for introducing the djembe drum to New Orleans and teaching the rhythms. To Zohar Isreal for teaching me the djun djun drum, including the tuning, repairing and making of drums. To the many instructors at the Kankouran and Tambacouda drum and dance conferences, and at drum classes in St. Louis, Atlanta, and Tallahassee.

The Costume Makers: To the people who helped me design and make drummer outfits. To Curtis Pierre who taught hat-making techniques, Abdoulaye "Papa" Camara for teaching how to make items using cowrie shells, and Peggy Irons who made the first outfits for the drum section in 1994.

To Ongoing Inspiration: To James Landry for helping me find the tribe. To Kenneth "AFRO" Williams for his encouragement to play for the tribe, and our Mardi Gras day jam sessions. And to Collins "Coach" Lewis for his spirit and knowledge of the history of the culture and helping to create new songs.

From Sylvester Francis

To my best friend, Clarence, who was with me when I snuck out of school to see my first jazz funeral.

To Jimmy Lewis for giving me my first Super 8 Camera in 1980.

To Samuel James and Warren Juluke for their moral support.

To my oldest sister, Elvera Touro, my biggest supporter along with my running partner, Collins "Coach" Lewis.

To my children: Sylvester, Clifford, Emmanuel, Santana, Daphne, Chrystal, Dwayne, and Domonique.

To my wife Anita "Lulu" Dillard Francis.

To all people who have helped with the museum, especially Henry Ker, Larry Bruce, and my brothers, Robert and Lawrence Francis.

To Joan Brown Rhodes for giving me Blandin Funeral Home to start the museum, and the entire Rhodes family for believing in it.

To the Neighborhood Watch, especially Brison and Marion Colbert.

To the New Orleans Jazz and Heritage Fest for inviting me to exhibit for more than 30 years.

To Charbonnet Funeral Home for helping with the horse and buggy for the All Saints' day parade every year.

To all my club members in the Gentlemen of Leisure Social & Pleasure Club.

To Tambourine & Fan. Thanks as well to Sudan Social Aid & Pleasure Club for having me be their honorary grand marshal in 2014.

To all the people who have served on the Backstreet's board.

And to the Mardi Gras Indians, Baby Dolls, and Bruce Sunpie Barnes with the Northside Skull and Bone Gang for making Carnival happen at the Backstreet.

From Jeffrey David Ehrenreich

Collaborative projects require colleagues who know how to share, consult, to listen and speak. I have been privileged to have many who have helped to make this book and my work in anthropology possible. Richard Schmertzing—who introduced me to Michael P. Smith and his inspirational work on Mardi Gras Indians before my coming to live in New Orleans—has been my colleague and friend for five decades.

My enduring thanks are directed to members of the Department of Anthropology at the University of New Orleans, but especially to Martha Ward, to my other colleagues in New Orleans, including Judith Maxwell, David Gladstone, Helen Regis, Shana Walton, Lisa Katzman, Aaron Walker, and Claire Tancons, who have all helped to make doing ethnography and photography so much more rewarding, productive, and meaningful. To Sylvester Francis—creator of the Backstreet Cultural Museum—and Cherice Harrison-Nelson—co-creator of the Mardi Gras Indian Hall of Fame—whose works are at the foundational core of the Black Indian tradition of New Orleans. And, to Rev. David "Goat" Carson, who helped connect me to his vision and to the Mandingo Warriors.

My intellectual debts endure to Michael Harner, Stanley Diamond, Edmund Carpenter, Judith Kempf, Solomon Miller, Rayna Rapp, and Bob Scholte, who guided me throughout my path in anthropology. My gratitude to Rachel Breunlin, my student and esteemed colleague, who has made collaborative ethnography her life's work, and to all connected to the Neighborhood Story Project, who worked tirelessly to

Beaded patch sewn by Collins "Coach" Lewis. Photograph by Christine Breault.

make this book project happen and to bring it to completion. Rachel was the driving force behind this project.

To Joan, Belinda, Cally, Nate, Peter, Kathy, Samara and Aviya, the family that sustains me throughout my days. And especially, to Victor Harris, and his extensive network of family, friends, and neighbors, to Jack Robertson, Collins "Coach" Lewis, Wesley "Drummer" Phillips, his creative co-conspirators, and to the other members of the Mandingo Warriors, who all have welcomed me into the incredible realm and community they have established. They have treated me with the kind of grace, compassion, respect, openness, and warmth that all humans need and crave. My heart and gratitude go out to them all.

From Rachel Breunlin

To my *ekip solid*:

To my ancestors. The ones I knew who have passed away: my great-grandmother Elsie and my grandparents Dorothy, Malcolm, Loretta, and Richard. And to the ones I have gotten to know through making this book: the English, Dutch, and Scandanavian settler colonists, and the immigrants from Belgium, the Black Forest, and Alsace-Lorraine. To embracing a different kind of family history that acknowledges the pursuit of peace and racial justice in reconciling the past.

To my father, Douglas Breunlin, who taught me about psychotherapy and the art of listening, and to my mother, Cynthia Breunlin, who taught me about social justice. To both of them for helping me move through changes over the last six years.

To Jeffrey David Ehrenreich for your mentorship into the world of anthropology, and trusting the NSP with all the years you have spent with Fi Yi Yi.

To the Committee of Fi Yi Yi for countless hours of recording life histories and going through pictures with me: Victor Harris, Jack Robertson, and Wesley Phillips. I love your collective artmaking, laughter, and deep friendships. When we were tired, the spirit of Collins "Coach" Lewis kept us going.

To everyone who contributed stories to the book: Jackie Alford, Resa "Cinnamon Black" Bazile, Bruce Sunpie Barnes, Kim Boutte, Reverend David "Goat" Carson, Marion Colbert, Ronald Dumas, Perry Emery, Jacob Devaney, Janet Sula Evans, Robert Francis, Sylvester Francis, Jr., Ricky Gettridge, Kevin Goodman, Christine Harris, Dijonaise Harris, Victor Harris, Jr., Fred Johnson, Chief Arvol Looking Horse, Asuettua Amor Amenkum Jackson, Darryl Montana, David Peter Montana, Sunni Patterson, Louis Pipkin, Al Polit, Ashton Ramsey, Renée Rome, Bernard Robertson, and Shaka Zulu.

To Sylvester, Domonique, Anita, and Robert Francis who opened the Backstreet's collections and archives for many years so that we could collaborate on this book.

To Abram Himelstein, G.K. Darby, and the staff at UNO Press: Katie Pfalzgraff, Ann Hackett, Matt Knutson, Thomas Price, Gabrielle Thorsen, Chelsey Shannon, and Glennis Waterman. Thank you for all of your support moving the book into world.

To the Department of Anthropology at the University of New Orleans, and our fearless leaders, David Berris and Ryan Grey, who have kept the ship on course with humor and great dedication. Thank you to Mark Pasternostro and Ebony Dumas for their archival work, and Niya Zulu for her interview with her grandfather, Zohar Israel.

To Cynthia Becker and Henry Drewal for being an inspiration for the hybrid medium of art history and collaborative ethnography.

To the NSP Board: Helen A. Regis, Troy Materre, Petrice Sams-Abiodun, Corlita Mahr-Spreen, and Kevin Graves for continuing to make us proud to be creating books for the city together. Thank you again to Helen Regis for being our series editor.

To everyone who supported the NSP and UNO Press's Write-A-Thon in 2017. A special thank you to everyone who supported my fundraising efforts on behalf of this project: Paul Chan, Emilie Taylor, Poppy Walker, Camille Lenain, Henry Lipkis, Jordan Hirsch, Keli Rylance, Faye Harrison, Kristen Conry, Eric Lassiter, Daniel Konecky, Ebony Dumas, KT Folz, Bonz and DeeDee Hart, Matt Sakakeeny, Helen and Carl Breunlin, Julia Belanger, Antoinette Jackson, Harold Toussaint, Bruce Sunpie Barnes, Katherine Doss, Candace Chambliss, David Beriss, Rebecca Snedeker, John Hargreaves, and Kathleen Sherell.

To the Thriving Cultures and Strong Local Economies programs at the Surdna Foundation for believing in the community investments needed to create collaborative ethnography. And to Judilee Reed and Jess Garz for all your support in creating the vision of the Neighborhood Story Project at UNO Press.

To Becky Smith, Daniel Hammer, and the archivists at The Historic New Orleans Collection. We feel proud to publish with you again. Thank-you to Michael P. Smith's family for sharing his photography with this book.

To Don Marshall and Scott Aiges at the New Orleans Jazz and Heritage Foundation for being early believers in this project.

To the Arts Council of New Orleans for supporting the day-to-day operations of our workshop.

To Gareth Breunlin for being an expert at collaborative graphic design. This is the book you have been waiting for.

To my sister-in-law, Kate Breunlin, for sharing late nights with this project, and having the NSP live in our family for the last 12 years.

To the New Orleans Workshop hosted by Helen Regis for reading early drafts of the book, especially Shana Walton, Martha Radice, and Sean Mallin for their insightful feedback.

To Max Omar, Simone Ophelia, Jasper Green, Nitza Agape, Lucy Belle, and Amelia Hart who have learned how to grow up with piles of books, drafts of stories, and designs around you. Thank-you to Abram Himelstein, Shana Sassoon, Nikki Thanos, and Leo Gorman for all of your help raising Max while I have worked on ethnographies. Our children growing up together is the great happiness in my life.

And to Bruce Sunpie Barnes who has spent time almost every day listening to stories about this book, editing and taking photographs, teaching, and putting on events with me. Thank you for being my best friend and partner through the highs and lows of collaborative ethnography.

Mardi Gras Indians suits on display at the Backstreet Cultural Museum. Photograph by Bruce Sunpie Barnes.

Table of Contents

PART I:

THE COMMITTEE MEMBERS OF FI YI YI

PART II:

COLLABORATIVE VISUAL ETHNOGRAPHY

WITH PHOTOGRAPHS BY JEFFREY DAVID EHRENREICH

PART III:

HOW WE DID IT

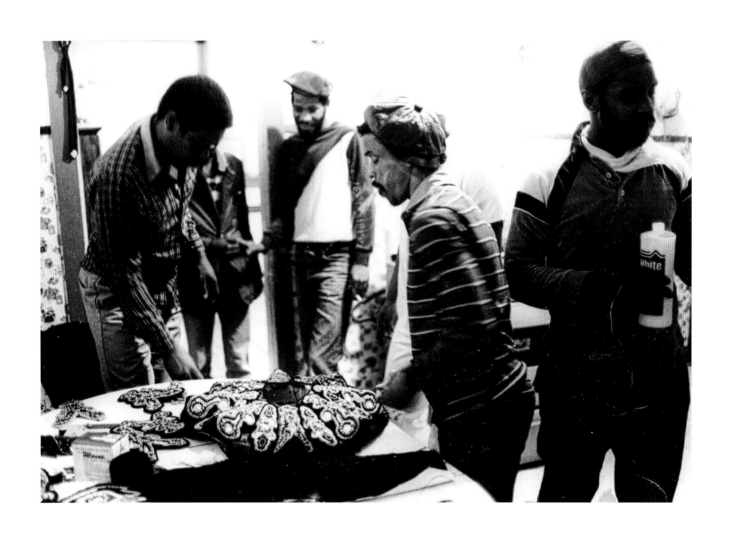

INTRODUCTION:
THE PAIN OF CHANGE

Left to right: Victor Harris and Collins "Coach" Lewis. Photographs by Jeffrey David Ehrenreich. *Previous spread right:* Close-ups of preparing Victor Harris's Mardi Gras Indian suit for Carnival in 1984. *Previous spread left:* Victor Harris, Brian "Eddie" Harris, Milton Smith (*holding apron*), and Collins "Coach" Lewis at Victor's house. Photograph by Michael P. Smith, courtesy of the Backstreet Cultural Museum.

Victor Harris, the Spirit of Fi Yi Yi: It was 1984 when Coach and I got cast out. It wasn't just myself; him too. We took it like champions. Or, he did. I say that because I was angry. I was upset. I was crazy. Man, I was out of it. Revenge was all I wanted.

Coach said, "Don't even worry about it. Them boys are talking; they don't even know what happened. We going to just do what we do and it is probably for the best." That is how Coach talks. That is how he would say it, so casually.

Collins "Coach" Lewis, Ambassador of the Mandingo Warriors: The spirit will be good and the spirit will be bad. If you do something to upset it, then it is going to get bad. As long as it is peaceful, then it is going to be good. That is one of the reasons why I do a lot of praying—to make sure that I'm prepared to be able to receive this thing here. Once I go to work, I go to work.

Victor: I wanted to mask for Carnival, but because of everything that had happened, I wasn't ready. I knew Coach would help me, but I never knew I had so many other people who would come to my rescue. The house was packed. We made some sacred beads with pearled eyes we called the Eye of the Fire. They were spiritual for us, and they would protect us. People were sewing day and night. Taking shifts. Sleeping, waking up, and not even going home. They were so dedicated to what they were doing. Boy, they were sewing, and you wouldn't believe how they were sewing. Everybody had a section like an assembly line. That is how the suit got done so quickly. They were telling me, "We got this."

Coach: Let me tell you a little something. It is hard to say that one man can do this. If you mask and you got family, they're involved because they understand that you are representing them. Then the boys in the community, your friends, they are all around you, too. They might not mask with you, but when you mask, they mask.

I'm talking about how we do it. At a certain time of year, we know we all want to be here together. You might not like it, but that is where you are going to be because it ain't about you, it is about what we've got to do. In the end, when it is all done, everybody is going to talk about, "I did that."

Victor: There is a picture Michael P. Smith took in front of the house on Carnival day. Curtis Lewis decorated it with Sylvester Francis. The front door had a sheet over it and there was a sign that said, "Flag of the Nation." I was still calling myself "Flag of the Nation," but I wasn't sure what nation I belonged to. I wasn't sure I had a chief. I look back on it, it was an extremely dangerous day.

A group came to my door. They were the same people I grew up around. We had all been together as one. We all knew each other. We knew each other's families. But now they were calling me out, saying I was a coward, a sell-out. I was on edge when my door busted open. It hit me so hard, it scared the living hell out of me. I jumped. All my door ever did was let me in and let me out. Let people in and let people out. My door never harmed no one. I lost my door now. I ran to the window. I could see this guy backing up like, "Yeah, I did it!"

Victor Harris's house on Annette Street during Carnival in 1984. "YPH" stands for "Yellow Pocahontas Hunters," a Mardi Gras Indian tribe in the Seventh Ward. Photographs by Michael P. Smith courtesy of The Historic New Orleans Collection.

I recognized him. It was a guy I taught football to on Hunter's Field when he was a child. I remembered the first day he got there, the other little kids hit him and knocked him down.

I asked him, "Why are you crying?"

"He hit me."

"Well, you hit him back. Stop crying. You make him cry." He got tough after that.

I moved away from the window and said, "I'm going to murder them." I tried to get out of that door, and they wouldn't let me out. It might have taken 15 people to restrain me. I'm saying, "I'm going to get them. Show them who the traitor is."

Coach said, "Man, you don't even know who did that, Victor."

"I know he did it!"

Coach knew I was right. He snuck out of the house. He went running to the big chief and said, "I would advise you all not to go close to Victor cause Victor is going to hurt somebody."

At my house, the suit was still in pieces. I'm telling everyone, "Get me my apron!" "Give me that!" "Sew this on!" "Let's get out!" I got people running behind me trying to catch up to me, sewing. Got needles still stuck all over my back. "Put

this together!" In an instant, I put it on. I left the house with a long handled machete and shield. The more stupid and crazy I acted, the more riled up my people were, pushing people out of the way until I got to Chief's block. I knew the tribe was going around picking up the rest of the members. Coach tried to send another message: "Tell them boys not to come around here." But they had to come back because I wasn't going to leave in front of Chief's door, and they had to come back to get him. They all got to come back here. Every one of them.

They had some water out there. I'm playing in the water, making signs with the machete. I'm look at the reflections in the water to make the water show me where they are hiding.

Here they come. They are finally back. One guy in the tribe came up to me. He was innocent, but he was with them. He said, "Yellow Pocahontas!" I splashed all the water on his suit. Went crazy on him. You could see his face: "Why did you do that?" But I didn't care.

Fred Johnson is a great friend of mine, but I can't see that now. I say, "Ain't nobody my friend because they don't care about helping." There were two shots fired. It doesn't bother me. I am invincible. With the eyes on the suit, I could see everything. I'm seeing things behind my back without turning around. The spirit was really truly in me.

I said, "Get them in front of me." One by one, I met them and told them crazy things. Even Jerome Smith's son, Taju—he is dead and gone, God bless him—who is my cousin. He is saying, "I didn't touch you." Still, I'm looking for the one little guy who broke my door. When I saw him, I jumped up like I was the devil. He wasn't prepared for what was about to happen.

He came in front of me. I'm doing a little sneaky warrior move. I'm getting a little closer in on him, and easing up. And then I got close enough to strike. He must have seen that machete coming up over his head. When I brought it out of the shield, there was so much a force it sparked. He had a rifle. He put it over his head just in the nick of time. It probably would have split him in two.

Now his neck is stuck out. I'm about to just come back with the knife. Everything started flashing, everything I taught him from the time I told him, "Stop crying. Hit him back." I can see every bit: *Click, click, click.* And as the images flashed back, I couldn't do it. I put the machete down.

Above: Victor Harris holding one of the beaded patches for his suit on Carnival day in 1984 with Collins "Coach" Lewis in the background. Photograph by Michael P. Smith, courtesy of The Historic New Orleans Collection.
Right: An Eye of Fire from the 1984 suit.

It was pandemonium. His mom and all them people were out there. People would blame each other for what happened. People fell apart. It was one of the worst things to happen in the Seventh Ward.

Coach: We could look at it a different way. It was time for a change. Now, how the change was made might not have been the right way, but it had to be done. Victor was on his way to greatness. Like anything else, sometimes you got to take and create your own greatness. Out of that change came the Spirit of the Fi Yi Yi.

Victor: When I was angry, I had nothing but anger. Anger can boil over the top and take you away from your own mind. Some people keep it in their hearts and never get over it. I didn't want it to destroy me.

Coach: It's great for a chief to make chiefs, right? Let's start there. Let's start with the Yellow Pocahontas.

Top: Victor Harris helping his son, Victor, Jr., get dressed on Carnival day in 1984. *Bottom:* Victor in front of his house on Annette Street. Photographs by Michael P. Smith courtesy of The Historic New Orleans Collection.

IN SEARCH OF HEALING: AN AFRICAN SPIRIT

The Yellow Pocahontas

Victor: When I was growing up, the Yellow Pocahontas had one of the larger Mardi Gras Indian tribes in the city. The whole front-of-town was Yellow Pocahontas. There wasn't no other tribes in front in the Seventh Ward but one. Just about everyone who masked with the Yellow Pocahontas stayed in that area.

Sylvester Francis, Founder of the Backstreet Cultural Museum: Back then, people were afraid. They always thought Indians were humbug, but my mama used to let me go out on Carnival day to see the big chief, Allison "Tootie" Montana. She would call me her special child and say, "Don't worry about that boy, he's going to be all right." I was a hustler and street educated from jump street.

Victor: On North Robertson, I watched my cousin Delores's husband, Melvin Reed, help the Yellow Pocahontas sew suits. Melvin was a little older than me, and he was the designer for the tribe. When I was a kid, this man made his own furniture. He worked at Swiss Bakery, and everybody who had a birthday, anything that was pertaining to that person, he would put it on the cake. It was a gift from him. After work, he sat outside sewing, and he watched me come and go in my alligator shoes. I'd make sure to wear a cool cap to match my shirts. He'd say, "Come over and see what I'm doing." I started going over to watch him. I started staying longer and longer. When he saw I was interested, he'd say, "Get this for me," or, "Cut that out for me." Little things he thought I could do.

Above: Sylvester Francis filming in front of the Backstreet Cultural Museum. Photograph by Jeffrey David Ehrenreich. ***Top right:*** In the 1970s, a crowd gathers in front of Allison "Tootie" Montana's house on Carnival day. ***Middle right:*** Spyboy Fred Johnson's Elephant suit.
Bottom right: Sylvester's wife, Anita, holding her son, Dwayne. Still images from Sylvester Francis's Super 8 film courtesy of the Backstreet Cultural Museum.
Previous page left: Close-ups of Tambourine & Fan flyers created by Douglas Redd, courtesy of the Backstreet Cultural Museum.
Previous page right: Victor Harris as the Spirit of Fi Yi Yi at his 20th year anniversary parade hosted by the Backstreet Cultural Museum in 2004. Photograph by Jeffrey David Ehrenreich.

Coach: It is like anything else, people want to find out if you're serious. They ain't going to waste their time with you if you don't want to learn. You be tested. You don't ever do too much talking. Can't talk and learn. You have to be an observer.

Victor: In 1965, Melvin said, "It is time for you to learn how to sew." I said, "Oh man, I don't know if I can do that."

"Well, you've been sitting here long enough watching me. You should know how to do this by now. I'm going to show you how."

All the beadwork I had seen before was beautiful to me, but now it seemed like I hadn't really been paying attention. Sewing took time. Melvin told me the easiest way to learn was to draw a line. He said, "Okay, I want you to sew that."

Left: David Crowder (*in orange*) with other members of the Yellow Pocahontas in front of Big Chief Allison "Tootie" Montana's house on North Villere Street in the Seventh Ward of New Orleans. Photograph by Michael P. Smith, courtesy of The Historic New Orleans Collection.
Right: Victor Harris in the Seventh Ward dressed as flagboy for the Yellow Pocahontas. He is holding Cayetano Hingle, who grew up to be the leader of the New Birth Brass Band. Photograph courtesy of Cayetano Hingle.

He showed me where to start: Stick my needle and thread underneath the canvas by this dot and come up. Put the pearls on the thread, and go to the other end. Make sure you have enough pearls to fit right to the end. Sometimes people put one too many. You get a whipping for that. After you put the right amount of pearls on the thread, you take the needle and go through the canvas and pull it underneath. Once the pearls are down, you come up from one side to the other, and repeat it. Once I learned that, he drew a circle. Believe it or not, circles are difficult, but they are essential to your suit.

On my first try, Melvin put his hand on the beads and said, "That is pretty cool, but see how loose it is? You need to make sure to get it a little tighter." Once I learned, he said, "Now you can sew."

I said, "You know something? I want to mask!"

"Now that you can sew, you can mask."

I was 15 years old. As Mardi Gras approached, I went to the chief to let him know I wanted to join his tribe. Tootie was a very intelligent man. A sharp dresser, too. I wouldn't say he boasted, but it could sound like he was bragging based on what he said about other people: "Oh, you got that raggedy suit on." He was a man of dignity, pride, and self-respect. He didn't communicate with people much.

Sylvester: Leading up to Carnival, Tootie didn't want anyone in his house. He didn't care if they talked to him or didn't talk to him, but they'd wait for him to come out on Carnival day.

Victor: There was no formal entrée into the Yellow Pocahontas. Chief didn't really deny anyone. He would tell you, "I don't want no trouble." I never understood that because the rest of the tribe also said, "You have to protect your chief." Why do you have to protect your chief if there is no trouble? See what I'm saying?

Fred Johnson, Anthony Hingle, and I started out the same year. We were road buddies. We played together, talked together. I was shy. I figured I didn't know much, so I kept quiet in the background. I had a little rhythm and movement, but I wasn't a good dancer and singer like Fred and Anthony were.

What I learned the first year was you had to take a stand. You had to be tough. I wasn't a challenging person, but people will push you around if you are not man enough to stand up to the challenge. It wasn't an easy thing to do. When you met another tribe, you didn't know what was going to take place. You had to be a warrior. You had to be brave. The other tribe is going to try to push their way through to get to the chief, which is like checkmate. That is why the spyboy is there, the flagboy's there—to make sure that nobody comes through. If they keep persisting? Well, you got to stop them from coming. This was my education because I was out of school by then.

A Tambourine & Fan flyer for Super Sunday created by Douglas Redd. Image courtesy of the Backstreet Cultural Museum.

Tambourine & Fan

Victor: Around the same time, the other part of my education began. One of the co-founders of the New Orleans chapter of the Congress of Racial Equality, Jerome Smith, came along and brought us all together. He saw us playing street ball because there wasn't a park in the neighborhood. A lot of times the police would come, stop us, and tell us we were going to jail if we played anymore. Jerome talked to everyone's parents in the neighborhood and got together hundreds of kids to stage a protest. We carried signs that we needed a park and marched in the streets. Moon Landrieu was the mayor then. When we got to City Hall, there were signs, "No Walking on Grass." Jerome and everybody said, "Look, you all just sit on it. Don't even worry about it." We sat on the grass nonviolently. Jerome took a few kids to the mayor's office and told the mayor how he had to go get kids out of jail for playing ball, and we needed a park. We named the park Hunter's Field after Tootie Montana's tribe, the Yellow Pocahontas Hunters.

Coach: Jerome grew up around Tootie as a child. During the Civil Rights Movement, he went to the United Nations with an apron from Chief's suit. He ran across a group from Ghana, and they thought the beadwork was from Africa. The cross-cultural hook-up was made. Through culture, we educate. You got everything in one package.

Victor: Jerome brought the spirit into a youth organization called Tambourine & Fan. Mardi Gras Indians were always there, but now we could talk about the history of the culture; about the origin of where black folks are actually from—the Motherland—and slavery. Tootie got so powerful because

Jerome saw Chief as the pride of the community and everything we did.

Coach: Coming out of the military, I joined Tambourine & Fan.

Victor: We started coaching at Hunter's Field.

Coach: All the street brothers. A lot of them didn't have no formal education, but they had wisdom, and they had the love for their people. People put their children in our hands. We had a chance to groom them. You would feel as proud as I am to see what the group of men who came out of that first class are doing today.

Victor: Tambourine & Fan gave me strength. It taught us who we were. It was a struggle, but it was never violent. We lived in a troubled world, but it was all about to build and to provide and to protect. The Black Panthers were the same way.

I loved coaching the children. They followed me. They called me Duck because I got down close to them to make little Donald Duck sounds and waddle with my hands behind my back. I would have them waddling during football practices, and kids would be falling all over the field.

We went through some journeys together. When the kids got on the bus to play a football game, we'd start beating on drums to bring out that fire. If there were even thoughts of fear, the drums would erase them.

Paul "Dusty" Honoré comes behind Spyboy Fred Johnson for the Yellow Pocahontas during a Tambourine & Fan Super Sunday parade on Orleans Avenue. Photograph by Michael P. Smith, courtesy of The Historic New Orleans Collection. Fred explains, "In downtown New Orleans, the suits were sewn with sequins and beads. All the designs on this suit were filled in with pearls. They come in different sizes. Melvin Reed and I would buy them white and dye them the colors to match the suit."

Coach: When he wasn't working or coaching, Victor used to be sewing. That is where I was at. During the period of Carnival, I used to leave home and move in with Victor. I packed a bag up and told them, "I'm gone." Melvin Reed was my teacher, too.

Victor: Melvin drew the designs for me, and I choose the colors I wanted and did all of the sewing at my own house. It was the greatest reunion of all time when we sat at the house and sewed together. It was the most fun time of my life. More fun than Christmas or any other time because the guys ribbed and cracked jokes on one another, and you would just laugh your heart out. They wanted to be there. Then there were people that you hadn't seen in years. You might have thought they were dead. They would come because they knew everybody was at the house.

Above: An exhibit of Ernest Skipper's record, "Shotgun Joe," at the Backstreet Cultural Museum. Photograph by Bruce Sunpie Barnes. *Top left:* Benny Jones, Senior and Janelle "Chi-lite" Marshall perform with the Dirty Dozen Brass Band at a second line parade in New Orleans. Photograph by Michael P. Smith, courtesy of The Historic New Orleans Collection. *Top right:* Ernest Skipper grand marshals the jazz funeral of Sylvester Francis's mother in Tremé. Photograph by Jeffrey David Ehrenreich.

Coach: I sacrificed to sit at the table with these people. Once they found out that I was observing, I started threading needles, pearling, and sewing sequins. You learn who was good at this and who was good at that. You sit down and you listen to the oral history so you can pass it along. Once you learn how to do it, nobody can take it from you.

Flag of the Nation

Victor: When Ray "Hatchet" Blazio stopped masking, everyone in the Yellow Pocahontas was asking, "Who is going to be the Number One flagboy?" Anthony Hingle was the other flagboy. It was time for someone to get to Number One, and he deserved it. I stayed out front on the battlefield. A lot of times other members thought I was showing off because I was so active. They'd say, "Duck don't want to listen. That boy have a hard head." Not just on Carnival, but throughout the year. But if I didn't feel like it was right, I was going to say something.

They kept saying, "Who was Number One flag?" I kept saying, "You can be Number One flag. I'm Flag of the Nation." Everybody kept calling me "Flag of the Nation." That title stuck with me.

Sylvester: Victor was a man who liked to follow himself. Everybody downtown made a suit like Tootie Montana, but Victor was different. He had his own style. And that might have been the reason he had so much power. Vic had his family supporting him. Men and women. Just the family was almost a hundred people. We used to call it the posse.

Victor: In the early 1980s, Ernest Skipper asked me to help him record a song, "Shotgun Joe." I didn't know him too well. He came up through Alvin Landry and Coach. They all were together at Clark Senior High School in the Sixth Ward. Skipper had the Dirty Dozen Brass Band playing the music, and wanted some background with the Mardi Gras Indian chant because it was a Mardi Gras

An exhibit at the Backstreet Cultural Museum dedicated to the life of Allison "Tootie" Montana, the big chief of the Yellow Pocahontas Mardi Gras Indian tribe, includes the sign "Chief of Chiefs" that Victor Harris carried during Tootie's jazz funeral in 2005. Photograph by Bruce Sunpie Barnes.

song. Coach and I went into a studio and jumped into some recording. My basic part was to do a chant and play tambourine after the music started. I would come in and say, "Flagboy! Flagboy! Flag of the Nation! Yellow Pocahontas! Downtown! Flagboy!" It actually sounded pretty good, like we rehearsed it.

Skipper was ecstatic about it, "Oh man, this is wonderful. This is great." I tried to tell him, "Let's use it as a demo. Let's see what we can do to add to it." He said, "No, this is it. I'm running with this. This is how I want the song."

Sylvester: On the record, Skipper wanted to do right by Victor and Coach. He put their names on the record as "Yellow Pocahontas." It was a mistake. Different parts of the tribe thought Victor put their names down as Yellow Pocahontas on purpose.

Victor: My little brother, Brian "Eddie" Harris, started saying, "Everybody talking about you being bad. They saying you sold out."

"What you talking about? What is you saying?" Sometimes my brother can get a little rowdy. He wouldn't let it drop so I said, "Let me go find out what is happening."

Sylvester: Before Carnival, more and more it looked like everyone was getting madder and madder.
Victor: While I was walking down the street, people were looking at me strange and talking. I said to myself, "What is going on around here?"

They said, "Oh boy, you messed up." I said, "How come I messed up?" They said, "You sold the tribe out." It was getting to me, "Look, boy, you don't know what the hell you are talking about!" I used to snap like that sometimes.

I went over to Melvin's house to get my drawings, but he was never home. That was strange. I could always catch him at home. Now suddenly I can't find him. When I finally caught

up with him, I asked him, "What is happening with all this?" He said, "Well, you see, I can't do it for you."

"You can't do it?!"

"I can't do anything for you anymore."

"You can't do what for me?"

"I can't give you no design. I can't draw for you anymore."

He was the one that said, "You and Coach went and made a song using the Yellow Pocahontas name and didn't tell the chief about it. That is an offense when you don't report to the chief."

I didn't know Skipper had put out the record; he didn't tell me about it. I said, "Y'all didn't even call me in so I could defend myself." They were shoving me away.

I went right to Chief and asked what was happening. He cleared his throat and said, "Well, those boys saying..." It seemed like a decision had already been made.

13

Spirit of Fi Yi Yi

Victor: After Carnival, I felt devastated by my anger; what I had almost done because of it.

Sylvester: At that time, Indians came out three times a year: Carnival day, St. Joseph's night on March 19th, and Tambourine & Fan's Super Sunday parade. St. Joseph was just a few weeks away, and Victor said he can't come out with the Yellow Pocahontas.

Victor: I didn't have a tribe. I came to a point where I said, "Lord, I got to understand why this is happening to me." One night, I turned off all the lights. I kicked off the TV. I pulled the plug on the refrigerator so it wouldn't hum. I unticked the clock.

I'm in the dark, and I put my back against the wall on the side of the stove. I'm praying, "I need an answer, Lord, because I'm down like I've never felt in my life." I said, "Lord, please let me know something. Please. Talk to me. Help me." I'm waiting on the answer like the Lord is going to say, "Victor…" but that didn't happen. Eyes closed with tears running down my face and I'm still waiting. The Lord ain't saying nothing to me. I just cried myself to sleep.

I woke up the next morning, and I was in the same position. People usually don't wake up feeling good. For some reason, I woke up, and I'm feeling good. I'm stretching and getting the kinks out, and I'm saying "Ya Ya, Ya Ya." I'm listening to the Ya Ya and I'm hearing the Fi Ya Ya. I said, "Fi Ya Ya." And my eyes bug open. I say, "Fi Yi Yi." Then I said it again. "Fi Yi Yi." The third time I shouted, "Fi Yi Yi!" with the stretch and feeling coming out of me. I'm shouting it out to the top of my lungs. The Spirit of Fi Yi Yi was born.

Sylvester: The week before St. Joseph, Victor told all the ones at the house—we're talking about fifteen people—"I'm coming out as Fi Yi Yi." He said it so much, when we left, we didn't forget it. We all took the name of Fi Yi Yi.

On St. Joseph's, Victor came out from the house on Annette. He came out in black, and he also had grass on his suit. No Indian, uptown or downtown, wore a mask and definitely didn't wear a grass suit with raffia. He came out with a real small mask, no crown. Tips, marabou, no feathers.

Victor: The spirit of my African ancestors had come to me: "You no more Indian. You are a Black man. You are an African man." I wanted to identify with my people. Africans painted their face, and they wore masks. There was something frightening, and also beautiful and spiritual about it.

Sylvester: That night, we met plenty of other Indians. We didn't meet Tootie, but Victor always had the respect for Tootie. I call Victor my chief. Victor still calls Tootie his chief. He never got too cocky to honor him. He always did say, "I want y'all to respect Tootie like you respect me."

Victor Harris wearing the first Fi Yi Yi mask in 1984. Photograph courtesy of the Backstreet Cultural Museum.

Collins "Coach" Lewis and Sylvester Francis at Sylvester's mother, Evelyn Francis's, jazz funeral in Tremé. Photograph by Jeffrey David Ehrenreich.

Victor: With the suit, I felt invincible, strong, untouchable. It was much different than wearing the crown. I started moving different.

Sylvester: Downtown, they were sewing big suits and big crowns. When they saw Victor's mask, everybody laughed. We didn't pay them no mind. One thing about the suit, it was extra pretty. The mask was small, but the aprons and neckline had extra beadwork on it. They couldn't say nothing. Victor was the talk of the town.

Victor: I was no longer feeling that Mardi Gras Indian spirit anymore. That was gone. I was dealing with the ancestors, the race of all people. Even though I still felt a lot of pain about having to leave the Yellow Pocahontas, I stayed on Annette Street. I wanted to be a representative of my neighborhood. Sewing was my contribution to make it safe and vibrant. I loved the coming together. As my children grew up, my backyard was full of their friends. I liked to give time, not just on Carnival day. It took a minute, but people started looking up to me as a chief. People sought me out to solve problems. I called my tribe the Mandingo Warriors. We were always together.

Documenting

Coach: I never did want to be no Indian. Wasn't ever my thing. Sometimes it is better to be a kingmaker than a king. Kingmaker has more power than a king. Without the kingmaker, there wouldn't be no king.

Sylvester: I didn't even sew. I think I was born to be a cameraman. In 1970, I started taking movies with Super 8 cameras. Rhodes Funeral Home, where I was working, helped me pay for the film. At the time, you had very few black cameramen. Not on Carnival day! My job was to take pictures, not knowing that you would call it "documenting." Truthfully, just doing it for us, but people started looking for me.

Carnival comes once a year, but second line parades and jazz funerals happen all the time. If they had a funeral, Rhodes Funeral Home let me off to film it. Coach went with me, even when we went to sit at the church, and they don't have one. You know, we just thought they were going to have one! We caught so many because we used to read the paper.

Victor: Every morning, Coach is gonna get up, and he's going to want some coffee, a cigarette, and the newspaper. He's going to sit down and read everything. It's going to calculate and accumulate in his mind, and then he's going to talk about everything he read.

Sylvester: Once I started shooting jazz funerals, I got the inside scoop, and the bandmembers called me, "Hey, we're going to play tomorrow." Coach knew even more musicians than me. Musicians always say to each other, "If you die first, I want you to play at my funeral." Coach and I used to talk about what kind of funeral we wanted, too.

Victor: Coach and Sylvester were two old timers. They would argue and fuss but one couldn't do without the other.

Sylvester: I started exhibiting my work at the New Orleans Jazz and Heritage Festival. A couple wearing dashikis were looking at my pictures on the wall, and the wife walked off. The husband called out to her, "Come back, come back! This is the powerhouse of knowledge!" Now, me and Coach? I'm the dumbest of all. I told him, "Hey bra, I'm the 'Powerhouse of Knowledge.'" Coach said, "If it won't be for Elvera or me, you ain't shit." If I told my oldest sister, Elvera, "I'm going to fly an airplane," she would ask for a seat next to me. Coach was like that, too. He believed in me.

Jack Robertson working on a Fi Yi Yi suit.
Photograph by Jeffrey David Ehrenreich.

Jack Joins the Table

Jack Robertson, Master Designer of the Mandingo Warriors: I was raised in the Third Ward near the Calliope Projects, the home of the Black Eagles. My friend Jerod "Rody" Lewis's daddy, Pete, was the chief. I used to see him and Howard Miller from the Creole Wild West during Carnival, but I didn't know what went into masking. It wasn't until I saw Victor's suits that I was able to focus on it. This was in the early 1980s. I was working at Charity Hospital and met a dude named Fred Williams. We call him Redhead. He stayed around the corner from Victor in the Seventh Ward, and we got tight. When we get off from work, we drank us some beer.

Redhead knew how to sew Indian suits, but had stopped. He started telling me about Victor. "The man crazy," is what he kept saying, but with admiration. He said, "Look, come by his house." Red took me by Annette Street a couple of times to look at Victor's suits. I was good with my hands. My father was the handyman for our block and would bring me along to help him. He was a good drawer, too. I still remember him drawing me a world map for school!

One Saturday night when we passed by, Victor was on his way out. He was sewing the Green Elephant suit and had some designs on the table. As he left, he said, "You can mess with them if you want." It was just Red and me. I said, "Well, I'm going to pick this up." Victor had already outlined it. I said, "I'm going to see if I can do this." The patch was loose and shaky, but when Victor returned he said, "That look pretty good! You all ought to come back and I'll show you how to do it."

I kept going back and now I'm hooked. My mama asked, "You going to be an Indian or something?" I said, "I don't know yet. I'm making an outfit." I had worked at Charity a long time. I knew about commitment to work, but I didn't think I was making a commitment to masking.

Everybody had different jobs. They got people who sew. They got people who hook the suit up for Victor. At first, I was with the sequins people. When the hook-up men were called, there was nothing in between me, Coach, and Darryl "Wool" Lewis.

Victor: On our suits, you can see the way that we sew with the nuggets. Darryl "Wool" Lewis was the Nugget Man. He was in charge of looping and sewing beads over beads to create layers on the suit. We didn't use cardboard to have the beadwork stick out three dimensional like a lot of downtown tribes do. We use layers of beads to build out the work.

Jack: I soon realized it is not nice to work for Fi Yi Yi. It is not an ordinary tribe.

Victor: Coach had the mouth, which is how he got his first position: Commissioner of the Sewing Table. Big talk. "Victor, tell them boys to listen to me!" I'd say, "Coach, make sure you check all their work. Look at the back of the design and see that it's all lined up." The back of the design is supposed to look like the front of the design. You can see a pattern if it is stitched right. It may look perfect on top, but you could have a lot of notches and loose thread hanging on the back. Coach would say, "Hey man, look what happened back here. Look like you having a rough time."

Jack: After a while I told Victor, "I don't think I want to work with you. I can't go through all this trouble here. Everybody blaming me for stuff I don't even know. I'm trying to help." I told him, "I'm going to leave this alone."

Victor told Coach, "Leave that man alone. I'm going to take him under my wing, and he's going to work with me." At first, it was kind of easy, but as it got close to Mardi Gras, they were going faster and faster. I was saying to myself, "Lord have mercy, they are working me more now." I struggled, but I kept up with it.

While we're sewing, the house is a mess. Every night someone comes in. You tell them, "Look, we rushing trying to get our stuff out. We can't be fooling around." They still knock on the door.

The elephant mask Jack Robertson worked on the first year he joined FiYiYi. Photograph by Jeffrey David Ehrenreich.

The first year, I was exhausted. I was tired. I was tired of everybody fussing at me. But Carnival was a glorious day. When they came out, I felt good. Nothing fell off the suit. We paraded that whole day with two little bongos and tambourines. We didn't have nobody to drum. I played the tambourine. I don't know if I was good, but I was playing it.

We got home late at night. We came across Canal Street, and Victor kept saying, "Keep up with all the children! Don't let anybody get lost!" Back when I was small, the Krewe of Rex had a barn on South Claiborne close to my house, and they'd pull their floats on old time wagons. By the streets being cobble brick, you'd hear the floats coming down: *clunk, clunk, clunk*. My friends and I followed them all the way over

to St. Charles Avenue. The Rex gold doubloons were the big thing. It was hard to catch them. We'd follow them until they came back to the barn by our house again. By the time we got back, we were wore out. I had that same feeling the first year with Fi Yi Yi. Everybody's head was down trying to make it home.

The next year, we made the Golden Unicorn suit. We went uptown around the Magnolia Projects and saw Roy and them with the Black Eagles. His brother was outside of the bar-room. We were playing drums, and he went inside and told his brother, "Man, come out of here and see the suit this man got." He kissed the unicorn. He said, "I ain't never found nothing like this." I get a lot of satisfaction when people tell

17

Jack Robertson and Collins "Coach" Lewis. Photograph by Jeffrey David Ehrenreich.

me how nice the suit looks. For a long time that was enough publicity. People who didn't know me didn't realize I was sewing with Victor.

After Carnival, we went to Atlanta to do a show, and I told him, "The Lord inspired me to come down here to make a change." Victor asked, "What?"

I said, "I'm going to bring you out to the glory land, but you will have to take it the rest of the way."

Then I told Coach, "Boy, when I take this table over we are going to form a union, and you are out of here. You got to go!" He said, "You ain't never getting this table! Chief better not ever give you this table."

Victor: Over the years, Coach and Jack started looking like they were brothers.

Jack: Coach was my mentor.

Victor: They would be mistaken for the other, but there was a difference in the way they worked. Coach took the

work I'd put together. Once the framework was there, I'd say, "You handle it." What I learned about Jack is that he can create the work. He can design it himself. I gave him the authority to do what he wants to do at the table. "You design that." "You handle it. That's on you." When you can throw that out at somebody, and trust them to do, it means a lot. There ain't nobody else I'm going to tell to do that.

Jack: When I first started, the mask was like two hands stuck together over Victor's face. I told him, "We've got to design the mask to look like a full face." I had no idea how to do that, but we started figuring it out. Once I get the outline of the face, I put the eyes in it and work my way around it. I always try to fill-in around the mask. If we don't make a whole crown, it will be a half. Every year something is different about the patches, too. They keep getting thicker.

Sometimes I think, "Lord, is it worth it?" When I'm sitting there sewing, I don't get a chance to really look at what I'm doing. A couple of days after Chief takes the suit off and I see all the work in it, I say, "Lord have mercy." Doing this has all kinds of little blessings everywhere.

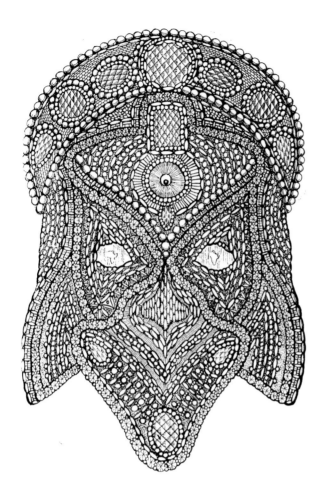

THE SPIRIT OF FI-YI-YI: A MARDI GRAS PHENOMENON

Mardi Gras. It's the biggest free party in America.
Parades. Costumes. Music. Food. And Indians. Yes, Indians --
Mardi Gras Indians.

The Mardi Gras Indian tradition of Blacks masking in hand
made costumes is over 80 years old. Traditionally the feather,
bead, sequine, stone and fabric costumes are hand-sewn, original
designs paid for entirely by the Indians themselves.

For many people, the Mardi Gras Indians are the most
beautiful and original aspect of Mardi Gras. The Mardi Gras
Indian gangs or tribes get together throughout the year to
prepare their costumes in sewing sessions and to practice their
chants and dances. Early on Mardi Gras morning they "come out"
dancing in the streets, greeting neighbors and friends, and
challenging other Indians.

Four years an important development took place in Mardi Gras
Indian culture. The Spirit of Fi-Yi-Yi took to the streets.
Victor Harris, originally a "Flag Boy" with the Yellow
Pochahauntas Mardi Gras Indian Tribe, was inspired to take a
significant step. Working with a nucleus of supporters, Harris
designed a suit which visually celebrated the "masking" spirit of
his African ancestors.

Most Mardi Indian costumes feature a feathered crown which
sits on the head. Victor Harris decided to create a mask
headpiece which fully covered the face in the African tradition.
Although the concept seems perfectly natural as a combination of
Mardi Gras masking and traditional African masking, the fact is

no one had thought of it until Victor Harris.

Additionally, Harris knew that his concept extended far
beyond masking. "It's like religion. We get together and sew
and sew, and sew. The thing is we're getting together as Black
people and creating something beautiful." Their creation is
called "The Spirit of Fi-Yi-Yi."

Patterned on traditional African motifs, the Fi-Yi-Yi
costume is entirely handmade from the leather boots to the full
face mask. Each section of the costume consists of various
abstract designs made of sequins, beads and stones surround by
ribbon, fabric and feathers.

The Fi-Yi-Yi gang collectively designs the costume.
Different members choose different sections to work on. Each
member comes up with a specific design. The designs are
discussed and once agreed upon, the tedious handwork begins. I
the final weeks leading up to Mardi Gras, the sewing sessions
sometimes last as long as 17 or 18 hours.

"There's no glue or staples or machine sewing. We do all
this by hand. Every bead, every sequein, every stone is put on
one at a time. And you know there are thousands and thousands
beads on this costume," comments Harris in describing the sewin
process.

Now in its fourth year, the 1988 costume will be green,
completing the four-color cycle black, red, gold and green whic
are the Fi-Yi-Yi colors. Beginning early on Mardi Gras morning
this unique contribution to the Mardi Gras Indian tradition wil
parade through the streets for all to see.

Audio-visual exhibits and workshops explaining the
significance and sewing techniques of Fi-Yi-Yi are available.
"We want to show the whole world what we are doing. From how we
sew to where our ideas come from, our mission is gather more and
more people under the flag of The Spirit of Fi-Yi-Yi," says Fi-
Yi-Yi Commissioner Collins Anthony Lewis, who is the contact
person. For more information call (504) 947-0514.

****

The 1988 Spirit of Fi-Yi-Yi Committee is Victor Harris,
Collins Lewis, Jack Robertson, Jude Barrier, Alonzo Stezenson,
III, Darryl Lewis, Yolanda Lewis, Fred Williams, CliffordHarris,
Byron Harris, Milton Smith, Sammy Graham, Alvin Landry, Bobby
Boutte, Mathews Boutte, Sam Griffin, Peter Louis, Paul Landry,
William Harris, Alfred Weenden, and Lionel Lewis.

Drawing: New Orleans-based artist Douglas Redd drew the detailed
beadwork of a Fi Yi Yi mask. Victor Harris explained: "That boy drew
that by hand! We all came up through Tambourine & Fan." ***Document:*** "We want to show the whole world what we are doing": The
Spirit of Fi Yi Yi Committee distributed a publication in 1988 that
explained the origins of their tribe and how they hoped to develop
workshops, documentaries, and performances. Documents courtesy
of the Backstreet Cultural Museum.

The Fi Yi Yi mask that Sylvester Francis helped sew in 1990 became the seed of the Backstreet Cultural Museum.
Photograph by Jeffrey David Ehrenreich.

Museum Beginnings

Sylvester: In 1990, Victor was running late, coming out in powder blue.

Jack: Victor had given everyone one piece and said, "Do your own design." I decided to use glass beads. It was the hardest thing I've ever done. I told everyone at the table, "I shouldn't have started this." You put a bottom layer, which was easy, but then you have to put a top layer. When you go between the glass, it can easily cut your thread. It looks pretty, but you're going to be a while now. I said, "We ain't never going to work with these beads again!"

Victor: And we've never worked with them since.

Sylvester: Me? I don't know how to sew, but I caught myself helping. My hands were bleeding from the needle. I didn't know how not to push too hard. I was doing small stuff, but I didn't sleep all night. I was living on Frenchmen Street, and Victor was coming out around the corner on Annette. I asked

my wife, Lulu, if she had everything set with my cameras. Did she have the batteries and tapes? She said yes, but when I got home, I fell asleep. I woke up, Carnival was over!

The next day, Victor and them talked about who they met, what they did, but I saw no Carnival the first time in my life. I followed Fi Yi Yi on St. Joseph's night and Super Sunday. I went by his house after. Just like all the rest of the years, the blue suit was thrown in the yard with a little dog back there just waving its tail. I asked Victor, "Can I have that piece with the mask?" On the top of the mask was the piece they let me sew. I felt like I paid for the mask! He told me, "Yeah." I took it and hung it by my house.

Every day, the guys from Flaming Arrow and Blackfoot Hunters came by to play pool in my garage. They saw the powder blue piece on the wall, and talked more and more about Victor's mask. That's one thing about Indians, they'll laugh and talk with you all the way up to the morning. But

Left: Sylvester Francis reading his booklet, *Keeping Jazz Funerals Alive,* while standing next to an exhibit showcasing memorial t-shirts for people who have passed away. Photograph by Rachel Breunlin. *Top right:* A photograph of Elvera Francis, Sylvester's sister and the former president of the Backstreet Cultural Museum. *Bottom right:* Sylvester's neighbor, Brison Colbert, holds a memorial Sylvester made for the ten-year anniversary of the Backstreet with photographs of people involved in African American performance traditions in New Orleans. Photograph by Jeffrey David Ehrenreich.

there's no kidding on the holiday. Come Carnival morning, if you are on the other side of the fence, shame on you. They know I call Victor my chief on Carnival day. I started begging Vic for more pieces. And this is how I started my museum. Nobody taught me how to make a museum. I learned myself from documenting the neighborhoods for so long.

Victor: Sylvester lived in the Seventh Ward. I've known him practically all my life. I thought it was best for him to get the knowledge and information before anyone else because he was in our community. He's the caretaker. He preserves all the culture and history of the inner city.

Sylvester: I had the museum at my house while I was working at black-owned funeral homes in the neighborhood. In 1999, Joan Rhodes asked me if I wanted to use an old funeral parlor the family wasn't using anymore for my museum. Blandin Funeral Home in Tremé. When I opened the doors, it looked like there was a service the night before. They still had all the tables and chairs arranged, and it had the smell of a funeral home. In the area where they laid out the body, they had the prayer stand. My friend Henry Ker and I used to work at Rhodes together. He saw me over at Blandin's and said, "Don't worry, I'll help you." He quit Rhodes and worked on the building from August to November for my first All Saints' day parade.

Victor: Back then, nobody would let you hold a suit. No one! But when the Indians saw my pictures, suits, and artifacts at the museum, they started to say, "Oh man, I've got some stuff I can put in there." They started thinking, "Wow, people could be looking at my suit, too."

Sylvester: My sister Elvera was the supervisor at a department store. She was already creating displays, and I used to get the mannequins from her store.

Top: The beginning of a jazz funeral leaving Blandin Funeral Home.
Photograph courtesy of the Backstreet Cultural Museum.
Bottom: Mementos from the funeral home on display at the Backstreet.

Victor: Sylvester provided a place for the suits to be shown but also a place for people to share their time and talk about events that happened. The Backstreet became the headquarters of the culture and the neighborhood where people felt good about who they are; everybody is somebody there.

Sylvester: People come by the museum and say Blandin is where their grandmother or grandfather was laid out. Some people take a while to come because it is the last spot they saw their loved one. Some won't come in here because of the memories, but they are still glad that it's the Backstreet Cultural Museum.

Long-term neighbors and supporters of the Backstreet Cultural Museum, Brison and Marion Colbert, on Carnival day. Photograph by Jeffrey David Ehrenreich.

Marion Colbert: Blandin was an old, old funeral home. My mother and sister were prepared there, but we wanted to have night-wakes at our own house. That's an old-time way. A lot of people wanted to be home with their body. Stay up all night long drinking coffee, and people come to visit. When they started doing wakes at places like Blandin, the all-night wakes stopped. Funeral homes only open up their doors from six to midnight.

A lot of people have fear about dead bodies, but I worked at funeral homes. I've combed their hair and felt their hands. Being with the dead can give you a cold feeling. I brought the flowers in. The families asked, "Where's Ms. Marion?" I tapped them on the shoulder to make them feel good: "Here, drink this coffee." It is hard to lose their people. Be with them people. Share your love with them. A towel, some cold water. Our day's coming.

When the pallbearers brought the body out of Blandin, a band would play over there, and the people would start second lining down. All that stopped when the funeral home closed down, but then Sylvester opened the museum and music came back.

I knew Sylvester when he was a young boy. I used to sit on his mother's step in the Seventh Ward. The prettiest lady. He had a beautiful mother. Sylvester was an independent person. He was smart, and he always was doing something. Brison is my last son living. He works as a plasterer, but helps Sylvester out at the museum.

Carnival is a day of happiness. It's crowded, honey. Hundreds of people are coming down, shaking the devil off. Dancing. I used to dance, but I can't dance anymore. I can hardly walk. On Carnival, I like to sit on the step and have my beads to give to the people passing by. Give them something to remember. Even more, a smile goes a long way. You never lose, you gain.

Bruce Sunpie Barnes, big chief
of the Northside Skull and
Bone Gang and president of
the board of the Backstreet
Cultural Museum, helps young
members Jawansey Ramsey
and Camarre DeVan get ready
on Carnival morning at the
museum. Photograph by
Jeffrey David Ehrenreich.

Bruce Sunpie Barnes, Big Chief of the Northside Skull and Bone Gang: When someone dies and people say, "They have moved on to a better place," it means that they have completed a cycle, and now they are on the other side where the ancestors guide and support those in the physical world. For those who remain, when you need real strength, you call on that. When you have a life change, you may have to rise from the ashes. Sometimes it has to be broken down before it can be reconstructed to take on a new life.

You could say it happened for Blandin's, too. When Sylvester started the Backstreet Cultural Museum, people would bring in things for the collection and say, "This was my grandfather's instrument." "Here is a picture of my great-grandmother." Most of the people who donated the Indian suits, buck jumper shoes, six inch heels—Lord knows it's a king's ransom to get your hands on some of those items—would also hang out here. They would come by and say, "Hey, they got a second line tomorrow."

It became an information center. It was more than just a museum, it was like a neighborhood cultural library where people came by to gain knowledge but also to give. It was a good place for me to go to school.

Sylvester: The first couple years, we stayed open for Carnival, and people started hanging. Victor and Al Morris, who was the Big Chief of the Northside Skull and Bone Gang at the time, used to pass by. My wife, Lulu, cooked and we gave them food and drinks. Seemed like an old funeral home would be good for a home base for skeletons. Al and Bruce Sunpie Barnes asked, "Hey, can we come out by y'all?"

Sunpie: The Northside Skull and Bone Gang comes out from the museum before the sun. At five in the morning, there are 150 people outside this door.

Top: The Northside Skull and Bone Gang's exhibit at the Backstreet Cultural Museum includes the original prayer stand from the Blandin Funeral Home. ***Bottom:*** Northside Skull and Bone Gang flag created by Bruce Sunpie Barnes includes the lineage of other chiefs who ran the gang. Al Morris's memorial button from his funeral is pinned next to his name. Photographs by Bruce Sunpie Barnes.

The Northside Skull and Bone Gang at St. Augustine Catholic Church's Tomb of the Unknown Slave: Seguenon Kone, Bruce Sunpie Barnes, Bruce Brown, Bakari Blackman, Solomon Israel, Zohar Israel, and Ronald W. Lewis. The memorial is on Governor Nicholls Street around the corner from the Backstreet Cultural Museum. The Northside stops here every Mardi Gras to sing and honor the unknown and unspoken voices of enslaved ancestors. Photograph by Jeffrey David Ehrenreich.

The Backstreet Cultural Museum was created through donations from people involved in the street cultures of New Orleans. *Left:* The exhibit on Mardi Gras Indians includes suits from Big Queen Jackie Alford (*the blue and pink suits*) and Big Chief Lionel Delpit (*purple*) of the Black Feather Mardi Gras Indian tribe. *Middle:* Resa "Cinnamon Black" Bazile, Queen of the Tremé Million Dollar Baby Dolls, in front of the Backstreet, where she has donated a number of her baby doll outfits. Photograph by Jeffrey David Ehrenreich. *Right:* A Carnival collage dedicated to music created by folk artist Ashton Ramsey. Photographs of exhibits by Bruce Sunpie Barnes.

Jackie Alford, Big Queen of Black Feathers: I donated two of my suits to the Backstreet. I used to look at the one my chief, Lionel Delpit, had on display, and knew I was going to sew a suit that would be good enough to be in there, too. When my chief was alive, he came up with the patterns, and we decided what kind of beadwork to use. Mr. Pernel (we call him Pretty P) masked with the Yellow Pocahontas and he drew the designs and put the suits together. Our job is to sew and wear the finished suit. Nobody can say they put a needle on my suits. Everything is hand-made by me.

Resa "Cinnamon Black" Bazile, Queen of the Tremé Million Dollar Baby Dolls: The baby dolls go back to the 1920s. It was a rebellious time: women wanted to work, they wanted to smoke, they wanted to go out like the men did. Different baby doll groups had their own style. Of course, everyone knew about the baby dolls in Storyville, New Orleans's red light district, but they had dolls all over town.

I knew I wanted to be a baby doll. I hung out with the old women to get the new news. Antoinette K-Doe, who ran the Mother-in-Law Lounge, asked Miriam Batiste Reed, who had been a Million Dollar Baby Doll from the Sixth Ward, to show us how to sew. They also had a group called the Gold Digger Baby Dolls. I went out with them when I wanted to get down and dirty and dance. That's what had me going on; these are the roots of where my own group comes from.

My style of sewing has a mixture of influences, but it's always been fancy. I created this suit in 2006. You can see the baby dolls in the lace, the second line clubs with the fringe, and the embellishments on my gloves and the mirabou comes from the Indians. After Katrina, it took me two years to be able to move back to New Orleans, but in that time, I came for Carnival and other cultural events. The black and yellow represented a dark tunnel into a brighter future.

Ashton Ramsey, Folk Artist: I'm an artist and an historian from New Orleans. I love to read to children at the schools and teach history with Tambourine & Fan. I also bring the kids over to the Backstreet.

I make collages about the history and culture of the city that have been exhibited in all kinds of museums. I donated this suit to Sylvester. Sometimes when I'm over at the Backstreet, I'll talk with the visitors to tell them about the different costumes. I grew up with music and tell them how I passed it on in my own family. I played with the Original Dirty Dozen Brass Band and my grandsons play music with bands in the city. Victor Harris's wife, Christine, is my niece, and my godson, Jawansey Ramsey, masked for years with the Northside Skull and Bone Gang.

Sylvester Francis's brother, Robert Francis, holding the 2017 Fi Yi Yi mask. Photographs by Jeffrey David Ehrenreich.

Robert Francis: You know, I am a quiet person, but I know how to deal with people. I started dealing with tourists years ago when I worked on Bourbon Street. Some come to party, others have heard about New Orleans and want to know what it is really about.

Our family has been involved with the museum since the beginning. When Sylvester first started, I painted the building and started doing tours. A lot of people tell me it's the best museum they've ever been to. They like it because they are looking at the real deal. When I give a tour, I can explain the sewing to them because I have sewn myself.

I started sewing Indian suits when Sylvester's daughter, Domonique, was a little queen with Fi Yi Yi and my nephew, Alvin, was trail chief. I sewed the patches and

Sylvester put the suits together. The first year they came out of my mama's house, I couldn't follow them because I was too tired; I had stayed up all night. The years after that, I walked with them. It makes you feel good to hear people telling that person how pretty the suit is and you are the one in the background who put it together.

At the Backstreet, we have the largest collection of Mardi Gras Indian suits in the city. They need constant care. We have to blow them out, shake all the feathers out, sew what comes a-loose as people come through and pull and touch everything. All the suits are on loan, and Indians borrow them for different occasions. A lot of times when Victor comes to get a Fi Yi Yi suit, I take it down and put it up when he brings it back. People think of the power of the masks. I know their weight.

Drums

Wesley Phillips, Master Drummer of the Mandingo Warriors: In 1991, I moved into the Seventh Ward on North Robertson and Annette. My backyard and Victor's touched each other.

Victor: Wesley stayed by himself. If he was alone, his drum was his wife. I could look out my back door and actually put my hand on the fence and feel the rhythms. I'm saying, "Man, those drums is in my ear. The spirit is coming to me." We never knew each other, but I needed him to come with the tribe.

Wesley: For Carnival, I usually played with Casa Samba in the Zulu parade. In 1992, they didn't perform so I was at home on Annette Street. I started hearing people beating on bottles, cowbells, and tambourines. They didn't have nobody with a drum so I thought, "Let me just play a little while and kill some time." There were so many people in the yard waiting. And when the chief came out, all the focus turned to him. People with needles and thread were with him to make sure that nothing on his suit came loose. The drummers and singers were toward the back. Within the midst of everything, it was pandemonium.

Jack: But we noticed you. You could play. We knew it.

Wesley: A friend I grew up with in the Desire, Peewee Landry, was out there playing, and he told me who the group was. I thought, "I'll just play till the gate." It took a little while. Then I thought, "Well, I'll just play down the street." I walked a block or two. Then Brian "Eddie Pint" Harris said, "Let's go uptown!" Before I knew it, I had played the whole Carnival day!

Victor: My little brother, Eddie, was tired of being around the neighborhood. He always wanted to "Go get 'em!" That line actually became a song with second line bands. Words you hear in a song often come from words people say on the street. The band thinks, "Oh, that sounds good," and makes a song out of it.

Wesley: After that, Fi Yi Yi got ready to do a Super Sunday and said, "Go get the drummer." They didn't know my name. That is how they started calling me "Drummer." When I first started playing, I laid back to see what they were doing. The Mardi Gras Indian chanting is based on an African-derived call and response energy, or rhythm. A lot of the West African drums are very intense. It is hard to blend it in with the singing of Mardi Gras Indians because the drums are for

Wesley Phillips in front of the Backstreet Cultural Museum with drums that he made for the Mandingo Warriors. Photograph by Jeffrey David Ehrenreich.

dancing. At first, I didn't use the djembe because it is very busy and talks a lot. It would drown out the words.

After I played with Fi Yi Yi a while, I got used to the structure of the songs and adopted a beat to go with the singing. Some of the singers like Eddie got used to the way I played. I started making drums out of metal cans and goat or cow skin because you can play mellow without drowning out the singing. As more people who were dealing with the sewing followed me, they started playing the drums.

In the other different musical groups I performed with, the drummers have costumes. In 1993, I thought I would like to have a drummer's hat with cowrie shells and horse tail when I went out with Fi Yi Yi. I asked Papa Camara, an African

dance teacher from Senegal, to make a hat. He showed me how to sew cowrie shells. I started making my own hats and showed the other guys in Fi Yi Yi how to sew the shells on Victor's suit. It came to be a full circle for my own musical practice with African drumming in New Orleans.

In 1994, the ten-year anniversary of Fi Yi YI was the motivation to create the drum section. I went into the mode of having outfits to match the chief. I bought some fabric, designed dashikis, and got one of my co-workers at the IRS to sew it up. Each year it's become a challenge to find African fabric to match the costume.

Jack: The boys uptown say, "Y'all have changed the whole second line for the drummers with your outfits."

Left: Jack Robertson wearing Wesley Phillips's cowrie shell hat in 1997. ***Right:*** The first drum section in 1994 included (*in forefront*) Wesley Phillips, Fred "Redhead" William, and Jack Robertson. Photographs courtesy of Wesley Phillips.

Victor: Wesley don't like for me to say what I believe about him because he thinks I'm putting him in competition with other drummers, but he is one of the greatest drummers I have ever known. He is one of the greatest drummers in the world. I truly believe that. He is modest about what he is saying. He is not going to say it. But I want him to understand how I feel about him and have him understand that I acknowledge him.

Wesley: Poetry, African drumming, Civil Rights songs, and Mardi Gras Indian culture blended together to create our rhythms. I draw upon these different experiences to create our tribe's sound.

In 2005, the Spirit of Fi Yi Yi parades uptown during Super Sunday with Jack Robertson and other members of the Mandingo Warriors. Photograph by Jeffrey David Ehrenreich.

Left: Self-portrait by Jeffrey David Ehrenreich during his fieldwork among the Awá-Coaiquer in Ecuador in the 1970s. *Right:* Jeffrey David Ehrenreich photographing on Henriette Delille Street between the Backstreet Cultural Museum and St. Augustine Catholic Church. Photograph by Bruce Sunpie Barnes.

Photography

Victor: As Fi Yi Yi, we've always been determined to do things for ourselves. I told the committee, "We should have our own cameraman to take pictures around the table, and every event that we go to." I dreamt of yearbooks like you have in school. A Fi Yi Yi book of designs. But we never got around to it. And then we met Jeffrey.

Jeffrey David Ehrenreich, Official Photographer of the Mandingo Warriors: When I first came to New Orleans, I was an old-school ethnographer doing research with tribal people in Amazonia. I had a lot to learn about the city, but the first time I encountered Victor is still clear as a bell. He was standing by himself, taking off his suit, and I could see how he was slowly turning back into a regular person. He was loading the suit into his car and it was different from the other Indians. I said to myself, "That's African!" I took a few photographs that I don't think I'll ever find. A short time later, I saw him at the Backstreet Cultural Museum. Again, he struck me instantly. I could see something shamanic was a driving force.

Victor: I become the Mardi Gras preacher. It's a calling. It attracts the people. I love the gathering, whether it is a group of people I grew up with or a flock of photographers I've

never seen before. The vibration from the suit makes people want to touch Fi Yi Yi. They really have strong feelings for that. Sometimes they want to touch me or the suit, sometimes they want to take a picture, and sometimes they want to do both.

Jeffrey: My introduction to Mardi Gras Indians happened through photographs. I came to New Orleans in 1999 to be the chair of the Department of Anthropology at the University of New Orleans. I was familiar with the photographs of Michael P. Smith. Looking at the passionate expressions and poses in his images of spiritual churches, Mardi Gras Indians, and second lines left a tremendous impression on me.

Coach: Michael P. Smith was a good friend of mine. Part of his book, *Spirit World,* comes from sitting down on the floor in Victor's house photographing us in 1984, the year Victor became Fi Yi Yi.

Victor: Back then, we didn't have white folks coming into the houses, taking pictures. Truthfully, I didn't know how Michael got there in 1984. It was a shock to me. But after I was put out of the Yellow Pocahontas, some of the ways the

We wait
with bated breath and high
hopes
all to see the chief.
Not even a touch
but just a glimpse of his
garment
and all will be well.
With every stich
every sacred motion
every holy hymn and chant
we are reminded:
Those Who Have Gone Before
are living
are here
are pounding pavement, just
like us.
And they, too, are steeping in
excitement and longing
for a glimpse.

-Sunni Patterson

Top: Poet Sunni Patterson photographing the Spirit of Fi Yi Yi. ***Bottom:*** A long-time neighbor on North Robertson, Muriel Neves, greets Victor Harris on Carnival morning. Over the years, her son, Ricky, has joined the sewing table. Photographs by Jeffrey David Ehrenreich.

Top: Victor Harris pauses for photographs on St. Joseph's night.
Bottom: Cinnamon Black, as Fi Yi Yi's Voodoo Baby Doll Second Queen, pushes a crowd of photographers back as the group parades on Super Sunday. Photographs by Jeffrey David Ehrenreich.

organization had done things didn't matter to me anymore. Now I'm on my own to the point where I'm not going to be controlled by anyone. Let it be known.

Coach: I thought we got to take and present what we've done. To do that, you've got to take and give yourself to somebody else. Once they document something, you don't have no control.

Jeffrey: That is, if the documenter doesn't create room at their own table.

Coach: Sometimes you've got to utilize and not always be used.

Victor: Coach always said, "You scratch my back, I'll scratch yours."

Coach: In 1994, Michael paid the price. He really took a whipping—literally took a whipping—for publishing more pictures in his book, *Mardi Gras Indians.* People felt like they hadn't been asked if he could publish the photographs of them. We felt sorry for him.

Jeffrey: Michael was an industrial photographer, but in his free time he photographed Black performance traditions. I know that different Indians had different takes on Michael and what they did or didn't get out of it. I made the judgment that he was not like some of the other photographers who were taking pictures and selling them for money without any reciprocity.

Victor: Michael P. Smith was just a one-time thing. It wasn't like he was always there. But Jeffrey has been a determined person. He was going to get in one way or another. We welcomed him. He said there was something about the spirit that we had that he had to get close to us.

Jeffrey: To work with Fi Yi Yi, I had to learn how to photograph in this complicated environment.

Wesley: There are a lot of dynamics with photographers on the street. I don't like them crowded up all in front of you.

Victor: The wildman and spyboy of the tribe say, "Open up! Get out the way!" to push the crowd of people closing in on us. It's also why you might see me doing a lot of crazy things. I'm making people get the hell out of the way.

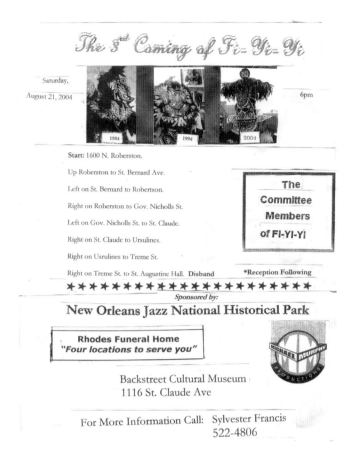

Left: A route sheet created by Sylvester Francis for the Spirit of Fi Yi Yi and the Mandingo Warriors' 20th anniversary parade includes a collage of images from the 1984, 1994, and 2004 suits created by the Committee Members of Fi Yi Yi. Image courtesy of the Backstreet Cultural Museum. *Top right:* The anniversary parade passes by St. Augustine Catholic Church and the Backstreet Cultural Museum, which are located on the same block of Henriette Delille Street. *Bottom right:* Big Chief Allison "Tootie" Montana of the Yellow Pocahontas and Big Chief Victor Harris of the Spirit of Fi Yi Yi and the Mandingo Warriors after the parade. Photographs by Jeffrey David Ehrenreich.

Jeffrey learned how to maneuver, but you've got those who don't know how to do it. For a lot of photographers, the ritual of the culture is something they don't understand. They all want to be able to get the picture, but that's not the moment to be there. They should not be there, honestly. Jeffrey got it bad. Jeffrey push the others out of the way, too: "I think I was here first, get back!"

Jack: "I'm their official photographer!"

Victor: "I got this!" He's been with us a very long time.

Jeffrey: As I got more involved in Fi Yi Yi, I realized that many of the events I was photographing were produced by the Backstreet. Much of the cultural landscape that I was interested in learning about and sharing through photography had been produced in other ways through the museum and the groups who supported it. My lens was influenced by this

collective vision and commitment to documentation. One of the first times our work overlapped was at the celebration the Backstreet hosted for Fi Yi Yi's 20th Anniversary.

Sylvester: Every ten years since the first Fi Yi Yi suit, Victor has come out in black. In 2004, he took one piece off every suit he had sewn to make that black suit. I put together a parade to celebrate it.

Victor: When I celebrated my 20 year anniversary, Tootie Montana came out to support me. I was very honored to have him there. Over the years, there were moments between us on the street. There were times when we met as the chiefs of two separate tribes. He never said much, but he acknowledged me. That was enough. At the parade, we gave each other a hug and Jeffrey took our picture. A lot of people know him as a legend, but I know him as my chief. I never stopped thinking of him that way.

EXCHANGES:
PARTICIPANT-OBSERVATION

Left: Victor Harris looking at the Fi Yi Yi mask created for Carnival in 2008. ***Previous spread left:*** A shamanic wing of a bird Reverend Goat Carson uses for the White Buffalo Day Prayer and Celebration, and a collage by folk artist Ashton Ramsey honoring Collins "Coach" Lewis. ***Previous spread right:*** Reverend Goat leading a White Buffalo Day ceremony in Congo Square in 2004. Photographs by Jeffrey David Ehrenreich.

Convening with the Spirit

Jack: Jeffrey, I went to a conference where you were giving a paper on Canal Street in New Orleans.

Jeffrey: Big meeting. The American Anthropological Association meeting.

Jack: I was sitting there, and some people told me, "All those anthropologists are nutcrackers."

Jeffrey: How crazy do you have to be to leave your own society to try to enter into other people's worlds? How disassociated do you have to be in the structures of your own world to make that an appealing thing to do? Many anthropologists are discontented critics. They are marginal to their own cultures. Welcome to my world.

Wesley: What's your family background?

Jeffrey: I grew up in a Jewish family in the Bronx in New York City, four blocks from Yankee Stadium. It was a mixed neighborhood in terms of religions and socioeconomics—a long way from New Orleans.

Jack: A lot of our people aren't originally from the city either. My mother was raised in Amite, Louisiana and my daddy's people were from Georgia. He worked for the railroad.

Coach: They tell me my great-grandparents were Indians on the river road. In St. Charles Parish, my mama and her sisters used to pile in a regular-sized bed and talk French Creole. They were close, but my daddy wanted to leave the plantation. He was tired of working for white folks for nothing. My parents wound up living in a shotgun house in Tremé.

My daddy's mother was raised on a plantation around Reserve, Louisiana, and she went to a spiritual church in someone's home in Tremé. They had services as early as 5:30 in the morning before they had to go clean up Ms. Sally's house, take care of Ms. Sally's children. They'd go to work for white folks and come back and have church again. Everybody be trying to pray. Ask the Lord to give them strength, knowledge, and wisdom to bear the cross that they got to carry because living in America at that time was real hard.

I used to go with my grandma to see them sisters in the white. I ain't never seen white like that nowhere else in my life! There is an altar in the corner with statues, fruits, and candles. If you were lucky, you might have a stand-up piano. A bass drum. Might be blessed to have a little two or three-piece choir. They were praying, singing, chanting, and they got the drums and the tambourine. I got hooked up into all of that.

Collins "Coach" Lewis singing at a
banquet at Sweet Lorraine's hosted by the
Sudan Social and Pleasure Club in 2009.
Photograph by Jeffrey David Ehrenreich.

Wesley: Music for me started in my living room where we had an old, little brown Magnus organ with white bass keys. I remember holding down the keys to give it that organ sound. My sister Beverly married a gospel singer from the Zion Harmonizers, so I would go with her to different rehearsals in the Desire Projects.

Jeffrey: Growing up in the Bronx, neither my mother nor father were especially religious, though I was bar mitzvahed, which is a Jewish rite of passage where you are given adult status. To me, it meant more in a social and cultural sense than a religious one.

Victor: I never was too much of a religious person myself. I was more a spiritual person. My mother tried and tried to make us go to church—Catholic. We couldn't understand anything because they were speaking Latin. Get down on your knees, get back up. I wasn't feeling anything there.

Coach: Ain't nobody choose your religion. Everybody serves their God how they want to. Religion is something that you don't claim. Religion is something that you live. It's not about you. You are about it. If you are about it then you don't have to talk about that. You see that.

Jeffrey: For me, as a secular Jew, learning has been very

much at the core of Judaism. To be bar mitzvahed, by definition, means you have to be able to read and write. It is based on the notion that you can become a participant in the discussions of Torah that are the core of the Jewish religion. It taught me that learning is a significant component of being alive and being able to convene with "God" and "spirit." That you must, in fact, prepare yourself for that.

Ways of life that are satisfying to human beings is what I'm interested in as an anthropologist. When I was growing up, my parents were members of a social club called a "friendship circle." During the week or on the weekend, somewhere around ten couples met for a party at different houses. The women played mahjong, and the men played cards. These were the people I called "uncle" and "aunt." Their children were my "cousins." While there was only minimal blood relationships within the group, when I think of my cousins, I think first of my "fake" cousins. I went to camp and played ball, attended weddings and funerals with the people in the friendship circle. I miss all of that in my life today. For the most part, the cousins are scattered. The aunts and uncles are all gone. I could never recreate it. My adult years have been too transient.

Coach: When I was in elementary school, the city started talking about building a cultural center in Tremé around the Municipal Auditorium and Congo Square. They tore down our houses and took them people out of there. The majority moved to the Fischer Projects across the river. Some went to other projects. They displaced a whole community of people for a park that wasn't supposed to have no fence, and they fenced it in. They tore down history. Black folks' history. They moved the people, but they didn't move the spirit of the people.

The projects were nowhere in my daddy's plans; he wanted us to be successful. He worked hard every day for Boh Brothers with a shovel. When our house was torn down, we moved back-a-town in the Seventh Ward where the *passé blancs* lived. I was a child, but I still felt like, "I'm from the Sixth Ward. I'm from the Tremé."

Struggles

Victor: When I was young, everyone was invited in our home. The little we had, we shared with people who didn't have that. My daddy was a good guy, but he had a habit. He was an impulsive gambler who played Georgia Skin and Cotch. They were fast games where you had to put up a dollar every time you made a bet. He took chances on the little money he made to try to make some more money. When he lost, he didn't know how to come home to explain himself.

I couldn't stand seeing my mother struggle. I said, "Well, if there is something I can do to make it better, that is what I am going to do." I wanted to be an asset to the family. I'd say, "I ain't going to school. I'm going to get a job." I didn't say anything to Mom. I found me a job cleaning up and doing porter work at a little sandwich shop. Somebody came with a note to the house asking why I wasn't attending school. I got busted then. My family was against me not going to school. I was good at sports; they saw a possible future. But I felt like it wasn't right. I stopped going in ninth grade.

Jack: My parents stayed on me about school. At Booker T. Washington, I took up woodworking and mechanical drawing, but I never did go out into the world with it. Back then, you didn't see too many blacks in carpentry. It was hard to get in it.

Wesley: In the 1970s, all over the city, the schools were segregated and the Black Power Movement was growing. The Black Panthers were in the Desire, and when the police rode through the projects, patrolling, they would have their shotguns in the back windows. Our school pride at Carver was music. The band brought people in. I wanted to play, but I was afraid of not being able to pass the audition.

When I got to Southern University in New Orleans, the students were demonstrating. They had come up with a list of 17 demands, including a full-time nurse—you could only get sick on Tuesday since the clinic was only open one day of a week! They asked for more buildings. But the organization went pan-African, too. People were looking beyond the campus and the United States to repression throughout the world: they followed the warring factions in Angola and political developments in Mozambique.

At the same time, the saxophonist Kidd Jordan ran the jazz program. He used to play with the Sun Ra Arkestra and brought his avant-garde style of music to campus. I started getting up my nerve to sit in. I was taking business classes and started a poetry group called the Desire Poets. We played at talent shows and other youth programs. I remember playing to the Last Poets' lines:

> Bodies ripped, torn, and chained.
> Stripped of language, fate, and name.
> Never before in history
> has mankind suffered such misery.

The teachers said, "Cut! Cut the program." People weren't ready for it.

Coach: I learned how to sing a capella at Clark Senior High. I was the first one in my family to graduate from high school. That was a big thing. I was blessed to come out with three scholarships for singing. But I didn't want to go to college and read Shakespeare, so I joined the Air Force.

Daddy got mad when I went in the military because he really didn't like white folks telling you what to do. I did nine months in Vietnam. Even in the military there was a whole lot of racism. I fought the white folks in the mess line. I came out an aircraft mechanic. If I wasn't so militant, I probably could have got me some license, worked out at the airport, and be retired. But I was militant.

Jack: When I graduated, I knew I had to go to work. You ain't going to lay around. I dibbled and dabbled a little bit until my mama's cousin told me to come to Charity Hospital. It was the public hospital. If you didn't have any money, you could go there for free. She said, "I'm telling you, we've got good benefits. Don't disappoint me."

I started picking up dirty linen. I rose myself up to working over in the laundry department and wound up a supervisor. From there, I transferred to the maintenance shop, and they sent me to school to be a laundry repairman. I repaired 600-pound washers and 400-pound dryers. The folding sheet

Jack Robertson working on an apron for the 2008 Fi Yi Yi suit. Photograph by Jeffrey David Ehrenreich.

machines and towel machines. It was hot. You had to work with young people, and you couldn't tell them nothing. All of them were hot headed, too. I stayed more than 30 years until the state of Louisiana didn't reopen the hospital after Hurricane Katrina.

Victor: I would have still been working at Charity if they hadn't shut it down. I started in 1972 as a porter and a pot washer. Within 17 months, I was made a food sanitation supervisor. I was only 22; a young, black guy being supervisor was unusual.

I met thousands of people at Charity because it was a very busy place. There were so many people I took care of because they knew who I was. If someone had folks who were admitted to the hospital, they'd tell me, "My mother's there" or "My child's there." Every day, I went to check on people to make sure they were comfortable and to do what I could to help them. It was rewarding.

Sylvester: I was on the front line of death, and it changed me. When I first started working for Rhodes Funeral Home, I went to pick up bodies with my brother-in-law. From there I moved to cleaning hearses and limos, and after a while I got to be a driver. In my family, I was taught to ask, "How you doing?" or say, "Good evening." That's respect. But when I worked for Rhodes, I had to learn something different. By the time you come to get a body with the hearse, the whole family has gathered, and they are going to be screaming and crying. The hardest part was trying to greet the family when nothing good is happening in that moment. I learned to be

low-key. Most people are scared of funeral homes, so you have to make them feel comfortable. You have to have the compassion for that person's loved one. Rhodes told me, "Treat everybody like they are your own people, like you would want to treat your loved ones."

Radical Difference

Jeffrey: In the 1970s, I was working at a life insurance company as a market researcher, and enrolled in a graduate program at the New School for Social Research in New York City. The New School was the pioneer in the development of adult education—people who were working and returning to school—and that was me. It was also known for its radicalism. In the early 1930s, as the turmoil in Europe ensued, the New School created the Graduate Faculty in Exile and brought over from Europe prominent scholars like Hannah Arendt and Claude Levi-Strauss who were endangered by Hitler's rise to power. I drew strength from that history.

I had come to study economics with Robert Heilbroner who taught capitalism, communism, and socialism from a comparative perspective. But in the weeks leading up to classes starting, everything changed. I inadvertently picked up a brochure that described a new program in cultural anthropology. I had never read a word of anthropology, but I read that brochure and something instantly happened to me. In describing tribal societies around the world, I realized that the critical feelings I had of my own would be best accomplished academically through a comparison of societies as far removed from my own as possible.

Five minutes later, I made up my mind. At the time, I was married but it didn't occur to me to call my wife. The decision was crystal clear. I saw the door to the office of the chair of the department was slightly ajar. I knocked and slowly pushed it open to see a man sitting in the dark behind a desk. It was August. He had a scarf around his neck and wore a brimmed hat. A light shined on a piece of writing he seemed to be editing. When he looked up, Stanley Diamond's message was clear: Don't bother me.

Nonetheless, he stopped writing, and I said by way of introduction, "I have just discovered I want to become an anthropologist." I didn't know Stanley from a hole in the ground, but when we looked at each other more closely, it was clear that we shared a background. Stanley got his doctoral degree at Columbia University, but he went to high school in the Bronx. He was, as I was, unmistakably a New York Jew. As we looked at each other, I think he saw a potential son figure and I saw a potential father figure.

Stanley was a poet and a leading figure in Marxist anthropology who had done fieldwork in Africa. The anthropology brochure that changed my life was based on a collection of essays he wrote called *In Search of the Primitive*. Although "primitive" has sometimes taken on a pejorative meaning, Stanley argued, in fact, that the word was related to something he called primary culture that evolved in small-scale societies where there is an emphasis on cooperation, collective enterprises, and family writ large. Not just family based on descent, but community. The respect for individual autonomy and the community, the necessity of embedding work into the broader fabric of society: these were themes conveyed in the one page brochure. Not utopian, but highly humanistic.

I didn't know it would take me 15 years to finish a dissertation about tribal people in Ecuador. When I came back from the field, I met my second wife and adopted her daughter, Belinda. I taught anthropology and eventually learned how to be a single parent. Parenting, writing about a tropical rainforest far away from your life, and teaching in the cold Midwest was a hard combination. I wasn't used to how reserved people were.

Jack: When you first saw Mardi Gras Indians did they remind you of some of the Amazonian tribes that you had met?

Jeffrey: Not in an overt sense, but in a very important sense, yes. Your world, as I interpret it, permits transformation under these unbelievably oppressive circumstances that derive and come out of the post-Civil War era with all its Jim Crow bullshit. Mardi Gras Indian culture transcends material limitations. I can't be you, Jack. I don't have any pretenses along those lines, but I can see the value that comes out of what you are doing. It is worthy, brings respect, and other people admire it.

I have an opportunity for some of those things in my world, but I think you have more. My community is scattered. It is fragmented. You have something that most of the people I knew before being here in this culture don't have: an ongoing, fluid, dynamic community of family, of friends, of childhood connections that grow and change and shift, but it is all here. It is a limitation on the one hand, but it is a beautiful reality on the other.

White Buffalo Day

Jack: Jeffrey, who referred you to us?

Jeffrey: I did that all on my own in a certain sense, but I also did it in part through Reverend Goat Carson and Sylvester.

Victor: I met Goat through the Backstreet, too. He had learned about the museum and needed help with the White Buffalo day. Sylvester was the person who could get in touch with Mardi Gras Indians. If Goat needed somebody to help him with his parade, it was the right place to be.

Jeffrey: Goat developed connections to a Lakota reservation in South Dakota. He knew that there had been a lot of antagonism about the notion of New Orleanians masking as Indians.

Victor: For a long time, Indians thought we were making a mockery out of their culture.

Reverend Goat Carson: In 1994, I came to town as an old musician who was down on his luck and needed a place to hang. But when I arrived, I had a vision that there was something I had to do here. I had visions that I somehow had to bring the traditional back to the city.

I thought about the Mardi Gras Indians. The more I found out about them, I realized they emerged under the same prohibitions as Ghost Dancers. In the 1800s, the city didn't want them to do this dance, and they didn't want them to dress in these suits. I talked with two friends who were leading Ghost Dance ceremonies, and asked them if they would come down and invite the Mardi Gras Indians.

Reverend Goat Carson on the porch of the Backstreet Cultural Museum. Photograph by Jeffrey David Ehrenreich.

At the time, I was the barbecue king at Snake N Jakes Christmas Lounge. Everybody was loving my barbecue. Big Chief Smiley Ricks came in and left me a message with all these voodoo signs and Big Chief Tootie Montana's phone number. I called Tootie and told him my idea, and asked how he wanted to receive the invitation. He said he wanted a public ceremony to show everybody that we were brothers. I said, "Fine."

Many Natives in South Louisiana were infuriated with me. Their anger comes from the way their Indian identity was denied by the government. For a long time, the Houmas were listed as black. They were called derogatory names like "Sabine" and "Red Nigger." They had a real distaste for the Mardi Gras Indians, which they considered mascots. I got called to the drum: "Why do you think you can do this?"

I told them, "Well, I'm answering a vision. This is Buffalo medicine because it's the answer of prayer, and if I am right that I should do this, there will be a sign from a Buffalo nation. If I am wrong, there will be no sign."

We had the ceremony in Congo Square. Two or three hundred people showed up along with Mardi Gras Indian chiefs in their full regalia. This is August 27. It is hot! When you do a ceremony, you look for the medicine sign, which tells you whether your ceremony is on track. Our medicine sign was the dragonfly, which means brand new beginning. Congo Square was just packed with dragonflies. They were buzzing all around. I think sometimes you have to be outside of a culture to make a statement like this.

A few days later, we found out a white buffalo had been born on August 20th on a farm in Janesville, Wisconsin. Her name was Miracle. The prophecy of the White Buffalo Calf Woman of the Sioux was fulfilled. This is a religion based on the spirituality of the woman, the family, the children, and the tribe—in that order. When White Buffalo Calf Woman delivered the message, it was to live life like a prayer: be at peace and at harmony. The prophecy had said old enemies would put down their grievances and come together and share the pipe. Well, the Native Americans and Mardi Gras Indians were old enemies. To bring them together fulfilled part of the prophecy. I had been walking in prophecy and didn't even know it.

We decided to have a White Buffalo day. I got in touch with Arvol Looking Horse, the 19th Generation Keeper of the Sacred White Buffalo Calf Pipe. For the first one, Arvol sent down his spirit warrior, Dave Keith, to check everything out before he came. I had gotten this whole coalition of people together: everyone from Hare Krishnas to Rastafarians to lots of Mardi Gras Indians. We went to the Mississippi River and back to Congo Square. The musician Coco Robicheaux was our grand marshal. I was out in front like the spyboy. A huge storm was gathering. I looked at the drummer Luther Gray and asked, "We ready to go to storm?" He said, "I guess so." Back in Congo Square, here comes Fi Yi Yi and his group with their drums. Their syncopated rhythms along with the strong four beat of the native drum brought it together. Of everyone who participated, Fi Yi Yi and the Mandingo Warriors were the ones who were the most blown away spiritually by what happened.

Top: Luther Gray, co-founder of Congo Square Preservation Society, drumming at White Buffalo day in Congo Square in 2004 with Big Chief Allison "Tootie" Montana of the Yellow Pocahontas playing the tambourine. *Bottom:* Big Chief David Montana and Big Queen Ausettua Amenkum of the Washitaw Nation in front of St. Augustine Catholic Church before White Buffalo day in 2013. Photographs by Jeffrey David Ehrenreich.

David Peters Montana, Big Chief of the Washitaw Nation: At this particular time in my life, I was thinking about peace. Bringing out a new nation of the Carnival Indians, I was thinking about coming together with all the Indians in the city, and decided to sew the White Bison suit as a sacred symbol of our community.

Queen Ausettua Amor Amenkum and I decided that we would name our tribe Washitaw Nation. The Ouchita were indigenous people who were located from Canada all the way through Monroe, Louisiana. There are still mounds left to let people know they were there. We walk proudly in the name of Washitaw Nation. People of the mounds.

"It is vitally important that we recognize the beauty of our cultures as a source of healing from the violence in our streets and the dispair among our young people. The spirit of our singing and dancing has always been strong medicine for hard times. When we were called to South Africa by Ela Gandhi (Mahatma Gandhi's granddaughter) to do a pipe ceremony, we were told that it was the singing and dancing of the people that kept their spirit strong during Apartheid. Our cultures are beautiful. The regalia of our dancers. The songs and dances of the people are beautiful. In a healing way, it is time for us to know in our hearts that it is an honor for us to bring to our children the understanding and practice of this beauty as a way of life."

— Chief Arvol Looking Horse, from a speech on
display at the Backstreet Cultural Museum

Top: Chief Arvol Looking Horse at White Buffalo day in Congo Square in 2006. ***Bottom:*** Moments from years at White Buffalo day include Wesley Phillips and Collins "Coach" Lewis smoking the pipe; Victor Harris in 2004; and musician Cyril Neville, one of the founders of the White Buffalo Day Children's Cultural Exchange, performing at White Buffalo day in Congo Square in 2006. Photographs by Jeffrey David Ehrenreich.

On the Cheyenne River Indian-Reservation, where the buffalo roam. Jeffrey David Ehrenreich explains, "We asked if we could go to see them, and they said sure. We drive into this field, and get out. Very shortly thereafter, there is this huge herd around, and we're one of the herd." Jack remembers, "We got back in the car because we didn't know what they were going to do! They came all the way to car window like, 'Who that is?!'" Photograph by Jeffrey David Ehrenreich.

Cheyenne River Indian Reservation

Reverend Goat: In 2003, I worked with the Backstreet and a group of cultural activists to bring the Spirit of Fi Yi Yi and the Mandingo Warriors to the Cheyenne River Indian Reservation in South Dakota where Arvol Looking Horse lives.

Jeffrey: Reverend Goat asked me to come along to document the trip. I knew that this was kind of a historical moment. You remember these words, but I said, "You guys are bringing it full circle. You are coming back as Afro-centric Mardi Gras Indians who are now going to make the connection to Native Americas that have been applied in the Mardi Gras Indian tradition."

Victor: Being on that trip, tell me how much you learned about Coach?

Jeffrey: I learned about all of you.

Victor: Well, in particular about Coach. I would like to hear it.

Jeffrey: Let me tell you what Coach said. I'm driving. I'm sitting next to Coach, and he basically goes, "Okay, white boy, we got to educate your ass. Let me tell you what is going on."

Coach: My parents come out of the country together, and I had the opportunity to see the bottom half of slavery. I got in the struggle and tried to make things better for those who

were under. I found the poorest people in the community had to take care of the so-called prominent ones.

Jeffrey: It didn't take me more than five minutes to figure out this is somebody who came through the Civil Rights Movement. This is somebody who was pissed off, and rightfully so, about the ways in which the world has been structured and his place in it.

Coach: You know, we come today and we are still struggling because we gave too much away for nothing. We didn't demand nothing from what was taken.

Jack: I rode with y'all. Coach gave you the blues all the way there. I sat in the back thinking, "Poor Jeffrey."

Coach: I wore his mind out.

Jeffrey: When Coach was on my case on a regular basis, and everyone was singing in the car and they sounded like they were on the record, I had a feeling that I hadn't had in a long time: "I have returned to the Bronx!" I felt at home. After my trials by fire, I felt there was the possibility of entering into a deeper relationship with trust.

Goat: There are seven bands of the Sioux and each band has a sacred bundle. Arvol Looking Horse's band is the Sans Arc ("Without bows" in French) or *Itazipco* in Lakota. They shared the pipe of the Sun Dance ceremony with us.

Left: An exhibit at the Backstreet Cultural Museum dedicated to White Buffalo day includes Reverend Goat's ceremonial clothing made out of African mudcloth and a wolf fur hat. It also showcases a Plains Indian breastplate made with hair pipes: long, cylindrical beads made of bone that were traded throughout the Plains region. Photograph by Bruce Sunpie Barnes. *Top right:* Cheyenne River Indian Reservation. *Top middle:* Members of Fi Yi Yi and the Mandingo Warriors with Chief Arvol Looking Horse on the Cheyenne River Indian Reservation. *Top bottom:* Reverend Goat carrying Mardi Gras beads during the pow wow. Photographs by Jeffrey David Ehrenreich.

Coach: On the Lakota land, we felt the power. At the Sun Dance, we saw the warriors walk around, dragging buffalo skulls, blowing whistles, and looking in the sun. If you want to be a warrior, they take eagle claws and put them in your back. They hook you up, and you got to pull them heads until your skin rips. You ever seen a real buffalo head? Man, the skull of a buffalo is as big as a door. They do that, and they take a break. Everybody goes to the peace pipe. You smoke, and you come back out again, blowing whistles and looking in the sun.

Goat: We also went to a pow wow, or *wacipi*, where we were treated as a visiting tribe, and we did our dance and our songs. At the pow wow, they formed this huge circle of people. The drum was going, and they were doing the side step dance. It was gorgeous. We were sitting off to the side, and they told us, "No, you've got to fulfill the circle. Everybody get in the circle. Together." And then we followed the tradition and shook hands with everybody.

Top: Big Chief Victor Harris performs as the Spirit of Fi Yi Yi at the Flag day pow wow, or *wacipi* at the Cheyenne River Indian Reservation in 2003. *Bottom:* Lakota tribal members shake hands with Victor Harris and members of the Mandingo Warriors at the pow wow. Photographs by Jeffrey David Ehrenreich.

Victor Harris greets members of the Lakota at the *wacipi* at the Cheyenne River Indian Reservation. Photograph by Jeffrey David Ehrenreich.

On Carnival day in 2015, the Spirit of Fi Yi Yi meets a man in a wheelchair who had been sick with cancer for a long time. For a moment, he finds the strength to stand up. Photographs by Jeffrey David Ehrenreich.

Public Shamanism

Wesley: Tell me, Jeffrey, will you explain how you've seen us since you've come to the table?

Jeffrey: Some shamans are healers; they heal individuals in a medical context. But shamanism is also connected to prophets, prophecies, and public rituals. Shamans lead people in ritual blessings of fruit and harvesting. They help people with their problems. They do what, in this culture, we would call psychological counseling. What I see when you are in the street is a public ritual. You call it "going into the spirit." I see that as public shamanism.

Wesley: Looking at the people as we are parading, you get a sense of people's expressions—get to see we are bringing joy or happiness to them. You monitor the crowd and can get a sense that it is touching them.

Jeffrey: Public healing it is not just about, "I lay hands on you" or, "I give you medicine and you heal." The creation of both the mood and the environment in which transcendence of one consciousness into another occurs is a multi-layered phenomenon. It is not just, "I'm a shaman and you are a patient." Something else is going on. All societies and cultures deal with conflict. Those conflicts need healing. Racism is a social conflict. Lord knows it needs healing in this society and culture. Oppression. Discrimination. These are social ills. They are diseases not of the body, but they are diseases of the mind and the social fabric. My definitions of shamanism includes the healing that occurs when the Spirit of Fi Yi Yi and the Mandingo Warriors march down the street and a little kid sees you as culture heroes. You may be somebody that the little kid might even be afraid of. But he is going, "Oh man, I could be that someday."

Jack: People used to come by the house and say, "We come to get our blessing before Fi Yi Yi." I hate to say it, Jeffrey, but when I be sewing I ain't knowing what I am doing. When I'm sewing, I've got my dead ancestors' eyes. It is coming to me as I am doing it.

Victor: You know, Jack, they use the word retire, but you know. You in it for life.

Jack: Chief think we're still young, Jeffrey.

Jeffrey: That, Jack, is another story.

Wesley: Jeffrey, what makes you dance to our drums?

The Mandingo Warriors' drum section under Interstate 10 on North Claiborne Avenue on Carnival day: Collins "Coach" Lewis, Rob Salter, Jack Robertson, and Wesley Phillips. Vendors, Mardi Gras Indians, barbeque masters, New Orleans bounce music-themed photo booths, the Zulu parade, and countless other maskers and Mardi Gras enthusiasts gather under the bridge to celebrate Carnival each year. Photograph by Jeffrey David Ehrenreich.

Jeffrey: I can't sing worth a shit, but I can dance.

Wesley: He starts a little, then all of the sudden he's full on.

Jeffrey: Well, I have my dignity to preserve.

Wesley: The music be pulling you. If the drum beats are good, people are going to respond. And the drums will really lead people through situations. What makes it happen is the repetition and that's something that's hard to accomplish: Playing the same rhythm over and over until it becomes a cycle in a pattern. When it works, it can overtake you.

Jeffrey: I wish I could follow your drum beats. I can keep the most basic beats. When that drum starts going off, I can't do it with my hands, but I can dance to it. Often I'm in work mode, and I'm trying to figure out the best angle to shoot you from, but there are other times when that is not so important, and the music just takes over. There are many times I am sorry I am not able to participate as fully in it. I heard Wesley say that when I would speak the sounds, my hands did much better.

Wesley: People ask, "How you remember all them different rhythms?" With the West African drums, you really have to

be committed to that djembe. The djembe will tear up your hands. How them hands be, Jack?

Jack: I was playing, and when I got up the next day and felt my hands, I said, "No." I didn't get on that drum again.

Wesley: When you begin, your fingertips might have a tingling burn feeling to them. When you start hitting the drum, they won't hurt. But when you stop, you feel it. You've got to want this. You got to love the djembe. It is a powerful, powerful drum.

Victor: The kids in the neighborhood are drawn to the drums like our kids in Tambourine & Fan were years ago.

Wesley: They anticipate Mardi Gras because they want to come play with Fi Yi Yi. They know the beat we developed. It motivates me to keep it going.

Jeffrey: When shamans around the world practice, even if it is healing a sick person, it is often public, and it is almost always with music and dancing. Drums are fundamental, and I've always been attached to them.

Victor: I don't feel as strong when those drums are not with

The first three Fi Yi Yi suits created after Hurricane Katrina are on display at the Backstreet Cultural Museum. Photograph by Bruce Sunpie Barnes.

me. That is why I won't go anywhere without them. One time I went to New York to perform alone. I stayed at the Millennium Hotel in a luxury suite. I had everything, but I was lonely. I didn't like not being with the Mandingo Warriors.

After Hurricane Katrina

Coach: We were apart after Hurricane Katrina. It showed us a lot about ourselves: what we are supposed to be about, what really matters and what don't.

Sylvester: After the storm, Victor said he was coming for Carnival no matter what. He lost his house in Katrina. He didn't have no house. They came and sewed the green and gold suits by the museum.

Victor: I've had many reasons why I could say, "I'm not masking this year." I could have said it a thousand times. Every time I masked, it was a sacrifice. Sometimes it is the spirit that has been keeping me going because I'll say: "Well, I'm not masking," and the spirit will say, "Who told you you aren't masking? Are you saying it or am I saying it?"

Coach: If it wouldn't have been for the culture, the city of New Orleans wouldn't have come back. The culture people were some of the first ones back in this town. They came back when nobody else was coming back because they understood what was "spirit." We experienced it in South Dakota. We were jamming on a stage and the wind came up from different directions and circled us. You couldn't do nothing but do what you were doing. It was around you.

After Katrina, we had to feel the power of our own land to come back here. We knew the spirits of the ancestors were still here. After all they went through, the Lord blessed them and said, "Look here, that is your husband, but I'm your Husband. I'm going to plant this seed up in here, and I want you to nurture it. Just let it do what it do. I promise you, it ain't going to disappoint you. Let it sow because I got something in store for it." We knew if the ancestors were still here, the city was going to be all right.

Collaborative Visual Ethnography

Jeffrey: When I came back home to teach, Coach stayed with me on and off as he tried to find a permanent place to live. As we were rebuilding, I bought a digital camera, which gave me the freedom to begin doing intensive visual ethnography with you—a version of participant-observation that incorporates photography as a technique of recording and documenting culture. I didn't want to simply hit and run the way many anthropologists and photographers do. I wasn't interested in simply coming over to your house, sitting down with you, interviewing you, writing something up, and pretending that I knew something about you.

Victor: I know you have thousands of pictures of us. When I say thousands, I mean thousands!

Wesley: In the beginning, I didn't pay that much attention to the photography because I was concentrating on drumming. When you published the images of the trip to Cheyenne River in *City and Society*, your documentation of Mardi Gras Indians made me see the value in what we were doing. You were the first person who documented us in an extensive way. Sylvester had a collection, but you were doing something different. Whereas Sylvester's goal was to preserve and collect different items, yours was to put it into a story.

Jeffrey David Ehrenreich shooting by the Backstreet Cultural Museum on Carnival day. Photograph by Bruce Sunpie Barnes.

Jeffrey: In all that time I worked in Amazonia, I used to look down on anthropologists who treated the people they worked with as if they were members of the tribe. I have worked with six Amazonian groups, and I don't consider myself to be a member of any of them. But I do consider myself to be a member of the Mandingo Warriors. You are my friends. You are my community in New Orleans. I spend more time with people in Fi Yi Yi than with any other people in the city. The only people that I spend more time with are my closest family members.

Jack: Yep, that's true.

Jeffrey: What follows is the visual ethnography of the time we spent together. A dialogue between the pictures and the memories that surround them.

Victor: For so long we have gathered people together. Now we are doing it with Jeffrey's photographs. We asked the members and supporters of our tribe, as well as other Mardi Gras Indians and people important to this culture, to share their stories as well. On Carnival day, when I hear them call out, "Fire in the hole!" they are calling the Spirit of Fi Yi Yi, which was created by the faith of so many people. I hope they feel themselves in these pages. And for the ones that aren't here anymore, I carry their spirits into the next suit.

2 0 0 6

Jack Robertson (*left*) sews raffia onto Victor Harris's suit on Carnival day. Holding onto the chairs, Victor starts transitioning into the Spirit of Fi Yi Yi.

Family, documentarians, and neighbors gather on Carnival day to watch the Spirit of FiYiYi come out on Annette Street in the Seventh Ward.

Victor: The first year back after Katrina, Coach started singing.

Perry Emery, Flagboy of the Mandingo Warriors: Coach had a heavy voice people use to sing the old hymns. He'd sing:

> Calling all the people
> to come back home.
> New Orleans
> where you belong.

Victor: As I came out of the door on Annette Street on Carnival morning, the destruction from the storm was still there; the debris hadn't been removed from the streets. But all those people we called were back. When I looked out the door, it was a shock to me. People were hollering and screaming, and I was frozen in time. These were people who had lived in the Seventh Ward. It was their first time seeing each other since Hurricane Katrina. They were holding onto each other. With the love and joy people had being back together, it seemed like nothing was wrong.

Darryl Montana, Big Chief of the Yellow Pocahontas: Victor has a lot of respect for the Yellow Pocahontas; it's real. We meet each other every year. When he passes by the house on North Villere, you know it's Mardi Gras! Fi Yi Yi and the Mandingo Warriors' music is the heartbeat of the Seventh Ward. When they come, they bring that noise. It is always a celebratory event.

Victor: My chief, Tootie Montana, died on June 27 of 2005, two months before the storm. 2006 was the first Carnival he wasn't with us. It was an honor to bring flowers to his wife, Ms. Joyce, at their home on North Villere Street. She helped him sew his suits, and even though she didn't mask, she is a queen to me. Sharing is the spirit of the culture does heal people. They feel good, even if it's temporary, and that's great medicine.

Top: Collins "Coach" Lewis holding flowers as Victor Harris approaches the Montana home on North Villere Street in the Seventh Ward. *Bottom:* Victor presenting flowers to Big Chief Allison "Tootie" Montana's wife, Joyce Montana.

Coach: After the storm, I didn't have anywhere to live in New Orleans. I came back for Carnival, but then went back to Raleigh, North Carolina. Reverend Goat said the White Buffalo Day Children's Cultural Exchange wanted to do another exchange with First Nations in Arizona, but I didn't have any way to get back to the city. Jeffrey bought my ticket to get back to New Orleans so I could go with everyone. We went to visit the Hopi, Dené (Navajo), and the Yavapai-Prescott.

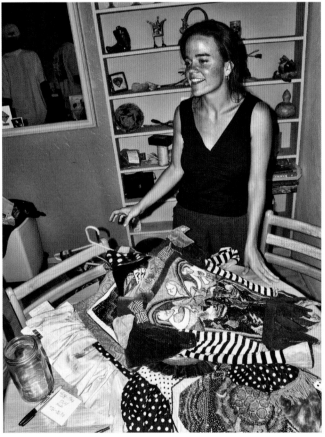

Top: Children from the Hopi Reservation in Arizona play basketball with Big Queen Kim Boutte and young members of the Mandingo Warriors.
Bottom left: Elizabeth Newman shares the beadwork she and Jacob Devaney sewed for their clown suits after visiting with Tootie and Joyce Montana in New Orleans. *Bottom right:* Ruben Saufkie explains a kachina doll to Jack Robertson and Kim Boutte at his home on the Hopi Reservation.

Ruben Saufkie and his children listen to members of Fi Yi Yi drum during a walk through the Hopi's traditional land.

Reverend Goat: I talked with Jacob Devaney and Elizabeth Newman, who are professional clowns, about organizing the cultural exhange. They worked with children on the Hopi Reservation.

Jacob Devaney: When Goat first invited us to New Orleans, we met with Tootie and Joyce Montana and sang an ancient Norse butterfly song, which is about the migration of people around the world. At the time, I didn't know anything about Black Indians, but Tootie wouldn't stop telling us about his suits. After that, Elizabeth and I hand beaded our clown suits. When Goat said he wanted to bring Fi Yi Yi to Arizona, we said we would help.

Reverend Goat: Clowns are really significant in Hopi culture. A priest cannot speak to the people unless there is a clown sitting next to him making fun of everything he says because the clown represents the people.

Jacob: When I assume that character, I am giving myself to the clown, the archetype. I was taught to let the spirits move through me. Don't be compelled by my own social sense of self. In some ways, Reverend Goat is like this, too. He is a real trickster, and can be this crazy-silly goat, but he has dream medicine, too.

Top: The Spirit of Fi Yi Yi and the Mandingo Warriors help clean an important water source in Hopi. ***Bottom left:*** Jacob Devaney performing at the Third Mesa Cultural Center. ***Bottom right:*** Victor Harris as the Spirit of Fi Yi Yi giving feathers to young children during his performance.

Jack: In Hopi, they brought us up in the mountains so high to show us some fresh water coming out of the ground. Ruben would go there to clean and bless it, so he took us with him. Now his children were running up and down while we were holding onto rocks. It was rough getting to it. We had to go down to where the pond was, and then climb back up.

Jacob: When Fi Yi Yi arrived, it was the beginning of the monsoon season, but still dry. We went to the Third Mesa to do a performance at the cultural center. The Hopi welcomed us with the Eagle Dance. The Eagle brings the rain, takes the prayers, and brings it to Creator.

Wesley: When people saw Victor in his mask, the children were scared to even look—they kept their hands over their eyes! Victor's mask looked like one of the Hopi Kachina dolls with the square head. That's why the people were skeptical because they didn't know what we were going to do. Some of the kids with us—Victor's daughter, Dijonaise, and them—went and got the other children to dance with them, and the parents loosened up when they saw the connection being made. Duing the performance, it started pouring down rain outside.

Jack: Afterwards, Vic let them see the suit and put their hands on it. They were holding the headpiece.

Above: The Eagle Dance at the Third Mesa Cultural Center.
Right: Jack Robertson and Reverend Goat Carson on Hopi land.

Jacob: There are Hopi stories that speak of previous earth changes on the planet. They say that some of the people were Anu Sinom—Ant People. Some of the Hopi went with the Ant People down to caves in the Grand Canyon, but some of the other relatives went up to the Star Nations. A new strand of people were born who were to create a way of peace that had never been experienced before. They had to get permission from the Africans—the oldest people on the planet—and they did. They had to travel around the world and make love to their enemies. By having their enemies' children there would be a way of peace in the future. The clans migrated all over the world. One by one, they started to return to Hopi. People of all colors are supposed to return. You could see the Spirit of Fi Yi Yi and the Mandingo Warriors as part of this return.

Coach: We had a chance to play at the edge of the Grand Canyon. The music brought the hawks and the ravens out when it was rolling.

Top: Wesely Phillips, Jack Robertson, Collins "Coach" Lewis, and Victor Harris on the edge of the Grand Canyon. ***Bottom left:*** Dené singers play one of the drums that Wesley created. ***Bottom middle:*** Folk artist and teacher Ashton Ramsey dressed for a performance in Arizona with "HELP" glasses written backwards in protest to the treatment New Orleanians received from the federal government after Hurricane Katrina. ***Bottom right:*** Teenagers on the Dené reservation get a closer look at the Fi Yi Yi mask.

Top: The Spirit of Fi Yi Yi and the Mandingo Warriors join members of the Dené in a dance at the end of their picnic together. *Bottom:* Young members of the Mandingo Warriors display their second line skills in Prescott, Arizona.

Ashton Ramsey: It was beautiful to visit Indian reservations. New Orleans was still recovering, and the air was so fresh in Arizona. Katrina was a horrific thing, and we wanted to show the other people what New Orleans was like before it. My costume showed different stages of the flood and all the help we got from different people. When we visited the Dené, we had a picnic in the park, and fed everyone. We performed for each other, and my grandson, Thaddeaus Ramsey, played the bass drum. At the end of the night, we all held hands and danced in a circle together.

2 0 0 7

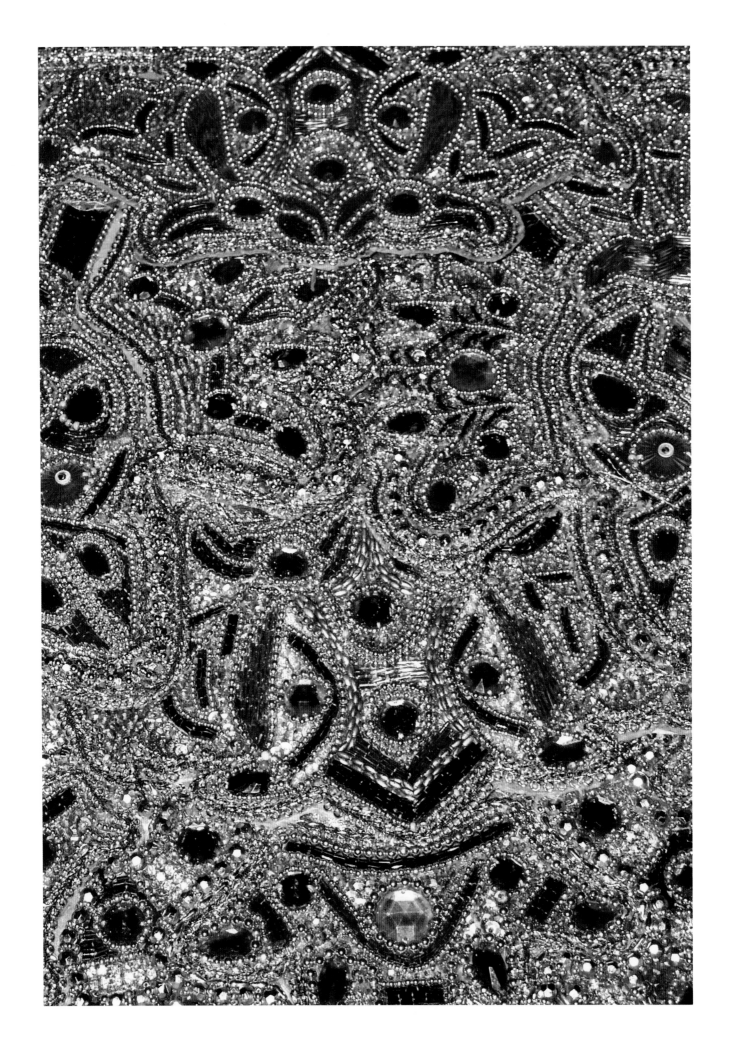

Rob Salter, Collins "Coach" Lewis, and Victor Harris at the sewing table. Throughout the year, the table moved to different locations as Victor, Coach, and other members of the tribe were still trying to rebuild their lives after Hurricane Katrina. For the golden suit, they returned to a traditional Mardi Gras Indian style with a Plains Indian-inspired crown in honor of Allison "Tootie" Montana, who loved the Indian song with the refrain, "My big chief's got a golden crown." Tootie Montana's last suit was gold as well.

Dijonaise Harris: Growing up, I knew my house was different from other people's. We'd have feathers and beads all over the place. I had access to a lot of arts and crafts. I learned tradition and loyalty. Family. Love. Passion, especially from my dad. He really loves this. When I was younger, he had an Indian room. I knew when the weather got a little cool, it was time for him to sit in the room and start sewing.

Christine Harris: I miss Victor during Mardi Gras season. I miss the quality time we spend together. I tell him, "It would be nice to see my husband." We'll be in the same house, but his mind is focused on getting everything done. The house is full; everybody's sewing and talking.

Victor: I've always loved the late night sewing.

Dijonaise: They had this big table and my daddy sat there with his friends. We came in to see what was going on and they'd run us out saying, "It's time for y'all to go to bed!"

Victor Harris, Jr.: Wool Lewis sewed even when my daddy wasn't around. He let us into the room when he was at work, and we could play with the beads and thread. He'd say, "Don't make a mess so your daddy won't know." We'd listen for his whistle. On a Friday night, when he would get off the bus from Charity Hospital, the sound of the whistle carried through the neighborhood and all of the kids would come running. They knew it was Fi Yi Yi. He would give us some money to go to the sweet shop or buy some Chinese rice. He worked hard to take care of us, and when he came home, he worked hard on his suits.

Victor: My daughter Angela knew how important it was to me. She would try to stay up with me, threading needles.

Dijonaise: Sometimes they had the door locked and they'd be in there all night. Just sewing all the way to going out. It felt like something spiritual.

Christine: I might get up in the morning and say, "Oh, you still up?"

Victor: The night before Carnival, there ain't no sleep. I love to be together just before that morning.

Christine Harris, Victor Harris's wife, helping their daughter Dijonaise get ready on Carnival morning.

Christine: I grew up in the Lower Ninth Ward. My mom's brother, Walter Ramsey, used to help out downtown Indians like Ivory Turner, and her other brother, Ashton, is an artist. When I was young, I woke up early to follow the Indians. Five o'clock in the morning, we'd put on our bandanas and go house-to-house all the way to the Seventh Ward where we would look for my daddy's mama, Big Queen Anita. She was one of the original baby dolls and the queen of the Eighth Ward Hunters. Still, I never thought I would be married to an Indian. My sons, nieces, daughter, and grandchildren have all masked. I help them get ready and sometimes go on trips with them.

Dijonaise: I started masking when I was three years old. When I was young, I saw my friends from school dressed in regular clothes for Carnival and I always had on an Indian suit. My fourteenth year was my cousin Becky's birthday, and we decided to wear regular clothes to walk around. It was cool, but the next year I was ready to be a queen

again—coming out, listening to the crowd call, "Pretty queen!" I know that's how my daddy feels when they call, "Big Chief!" It feels good.

Christine: I've met a lot of people through my husband. He's good with people. The reporters, photographers, anthropologists, professors, and art curators speak of us being such a nice family, taking outsiders in. But the way I see it is, "If you treat me right, I'll treat you right." It's that simple. I try not to get in the photographs too much, but Jeffrey feels like family to me.

I never masked myself, but each year I ask my husband to fix me some Mardi Gras boots. I try to get at least a pair of boots out of them! I enjoy all the other people in the tribe. I can say I am the queen behind the door.

Big Queen Cutie, Kim Boutte,
of the Mandingo Warriors
dancing on Carnival day.

Victor: Kim Boutte is the Big Queen of the Mandingo Warriors. She is one of my oldest sister, Emelda's, daughters.

Kim Boutte, Big Queen of the Mandingo Warriors: My grandmother had 19 children and all of us stick together. The family's always behind us.

Victor: Our whole family knows how to dance; that's all we ever did. Dance brought happiness, took away all the sadness. Growing up, Kim was around it. She has a lot of spunk, and she loves what she do. She is a very nimble person. The girl ran track in school and she still plays baseball. I don't think anybody can dance like her. She don't ever stop.

Kim: When I was young, I used to be with Tambourine & Fan and second lining with Big Jerome Smith, who is my cousin. I first started hitting the streets at Hunter's Field. Coach said, "Well, we know you with Tambourine & Fan. We are going to start being Indian." Fi Yi Yi said that he wanted some babies to be Indians. I said, "I want to be an Indian, too! I want to be an Indian when I get big." I started masking when I was about 15.

Jack: Kim is the main one who stayed with it. The girls we have usually march with us until they are teenagers and find out about boys. We have another group of girls and I hope they stay a little longer because I enjoy making their suits. If I can get Vic's halfway started, I can move over to the girls. The big queen's suit is the hardest one because she don't want to sew. I tell her, "If you going to be a big queen, you got to sit down and sew so you can look like a big queen."

Victor: Kim's not going to put her hands in the needles. She'll say, "You gonna sew for me, Jack, and my Uncle Vickie, too."

Jack: When I first started, she wanted to put me out of the tribe because I was from the Third Ward. Now she wants me to do her suit every year! When I start working on it, she'll say, "See, I told you, *you like me!*"

Kim: What I really like is meeting everybody. I like to have fun. They go to dancing and shouting, and we sing:

Who they talk about?
Fi Yi Yi!!
What they talk about?
Mandingo Warriors!!

I'm Big Queen, me. When we meet another tribe, I'm going to meet their queen. After I dance with her, I'm going to give her a little hug. Let her know I come from the Seventh Ward.

Left: David Montana, second chief of the Yellow Pocahontas. ***Right:*** Queen of the Yellow Pocahontas, Ausettua Amor Amenkum Jackson. David and Aussettua have gone on to start their own tribe, the Washitaw Nation.

Kim: From the beginning, Ausettua danced like she's been out here; like an old-time Indian. She is an African dancer and has her own dance company.

Ausettua Amor Amenkum Jackson: We organized New Orleans' premier African dance compay, Kumbuka African Drum and Dance Collective, in 1981, but I also got involved with Mardi Gras Indian culture in the 80s when I started playing drums with Big Chief Donald Harrison, Sr. of the Guardians of the Flame.

I live in the Seventh Ward so I was one of the people who would gather in front of Tootie Montana's door. I always wanted to take my picture with him. He'd say, "You ought to come mask with me!"

I thought about it, but I wasn't ready. In the spring of 2005, I shook Tootie's hand and said, "I'm coming. Next year is going to be my year." Wow, within a few months Tootie had passed away and Katrina rocked the city. I thought, "There go my chances." But then I met his nephew, David Montana.

David Peter Montana: For a long time, I played second chief with the Yellow Pocahontas. I would like to say some-thing about my beginnings with my father, Edward Alfred Montana. I picked up a suit in 1994 that he was working on and the spirit was on me to finish. That was the end of Edward and the beginning of me.

Ausettua: David didn't know me and the agreement I had made with Tootie, but he asked me if I wanted to join the tribe. I said, "It must have been meant to be." He taught me how to sew.

David: Like Victor, I have my own style. Most people downtown talk about three-dimensional design. I want to go beyond 3D to HD: Highly Defined. You can work on your suit every day and find something else to do, but at some point you've got to end the story and take to the street.

Ausettua: You have to wear white the first year you mask. I was sewing pieces until it all came together at the end. I couldn't imagine it before I put it on. These pictures show the first time Kim and I danced together as queens. Her movements are very buoyant. She high steps on the upside of the beat.

Big Chief Darryl Montana wearing his tribute to his father, Allison "Tootie" Montana.

Victor: In 2007, I honored Chief with the golden crown. I hadn't worn one since I left the Yellow Pocahontas. When I put it on, I kept thinking, "I don't know how Tootie carried them crowns!" You have to have something else in you beyond the physical strength to carry it yourself. It was a surprise to me that Tootie's son, Darryl, had made one as well. We have both honored Chief in our own way over the years. He's not his father. I'm not mine. Look how beautiful we were, for one year, together.

Darryl Montana: When I started this suit, my daddy was still living and I thought he would see it. But he died, and I didn't mask in 2006 because we were displaced from Katrina. It's the first suit that I worked on for more than one year. I traced a picture of my father, and built up a three-dimensional piece beaded with little seed beads as my tribute to him.

Alphonse "Dowee" Robair, gang flag of the Red Hawk Hunters of the Lower Ninth Ward, meets Victor Harris on Carnival day. Dowee has gone on to start his own tribe, the Black Ax.

Top: Victor Harris as the Spirit of Fi Yi Yi in front of St. Augustine Catholic Church on Henriette Delille Street in Tremé for Reverend Jerome LeDoux's 50th Anniversary in the priesthood celebration on June 3, 2007. During his time at the church, Father LeDoux often sponsored events with the Backstreet Cultural Museum like White Buffalo day, and hosted a jazz mass for Satchmo SummerFest, organized by the French Quarter Festival in honor of Louis Armstrong. According to Fred Johnson, former spyboy of the Yellow Pocahontas and president of Black Men of Labor Social Aid and Pleasure Club, "Father LaDoux was the most African Catholic Church priest we've ever engaged. He opened the church up to the community." *Bottom:* Reverend Jerome LeDoux giving the sermon at St. Augustine. After much struggle to reopen the church and include the culture of the neighborhood in the services, on November 1, 2007, All Saints' day, the Archdioceses of New Orleans appointed Father Quentin Moody as the reverend of the church, and relocated Father LaDoux to Dallas.

2 0 0 8

Throughout 2008, Victor and Christine Harris built a new house on Florida Avenue in the Ninth Ward. Here, Jack Robertson helps Collins "Coach" Lewis work on a collar for Cinnamon Black in a newly sheetrocked room.

Victor: A few weeks before Carnival, Jerome Smith asked, "I know you on that thread and needle so what's happening with that? We looking for you."

Jerome didn't know I wasn't going to mask. I was giving up. A few years after Katrina, a lot of my friends had passed away and the city was still recovering. Jerome wouldn't accept it. He said, "You coming, you masking!! I ain't even going to come out if you ain't masking!!" He took dollars out of his own pocket, and told me, "Take one of those suits from by Sylvester." Samuel Graham was a very dear, close friend. He would stutter when he talked. If I told him I wanted to go to the moon, he'd say, "Let me see if I can get a space shuttle." When he died in 2001, I did a service for him in a brown suit. I took that suit and worked on a new mask. Jerome actually kept my streak of continuous sewing alive.

Resa "Cinnamon Black" Bazile: For many years, I felt it in my heart that I wanted to make a connection between the Indians and baby dolls. I looked at the picture of Big Queen Anita in the Backstreet and I felt her Indian suit was like a baby doll. This gave me hope, but it took me 14 years to start sewing.

It was Coach who took me as his protége. In 2008, we really started sewing together. He said, "If you want to be serious about sewing, you are going to have to sew your own collar." I was scared to death. I would sew something and leave it at the table. When I came back, it was all taken aloose. He said, "It must not have been right." He was serious about, as he said, "architectural design."

Left: Collins "Coach" Lewis in front of the Backstreet Cultural Museum. *Right:* The big chief of the Northside Skull and Bone Gang, Bruce Sunpie Barnes, meets Victor Harris as the Spirit of Fi Yi Yi in front of the Backstreet. In the background, Ronald W. Lewis holds the last skeleton head created by the former big chief of the Northside, Al Morris. Through working on the mask with him, Sunpie learned Al's style of paper mâché. In 2009, Ronald produced a catalogue of his museum, *The House of Dance and Feathers*, with the Neighborhood Story Project.

Sunpie: When I first started masking skeleton, Fi Yi Yi was the first group to embrace me. Every time I meet them, I show big appreciation for their acknowledgment that I had a place in the culture. I have an African sensibility just as they do, and over the years we've let each other know what we notice is new about what we're doing. I decided to wear this top hat because it represents the old New Orleans tradition of the sextons, the groundkeepers who oversee the cemeteries, and it also represents Baron Samedi, the New Orleans spirit of the cemetery. My chief, Al Morris, agreed to the change. On the street, Coach recognized what I was doing and said, "Yeah, you've got to keep doing that." Their tribe always bring the peace, fire, and harmony.

Under the bridge on North Claiborne Avenue, Andaiye Alimayu (*with Sula Evans dressed in white behind her*) welcomes Victor Harris as the Spirit of Fi Yi Yi on Carnival day by pouring a libation as the tribe passes by. A Medicine Woman, singer, and artist, she is the owner of Shrine of the Holy Spirit (formerly King and Queen Emporium International) at 2500 Bayou Road, where she produces handcrafted soaps, incense, and jewelry, and sings with the vocal group Zion Trinity.

Andaiye Alimayu: In this city, it is better to be a chief than an elected official because you have more influence in your neighborhood.

Some of the first things I remember as a child in the 1970s was Tambourine & Fan's campaign, "Dope Is Death." With the introduction of crack cocaine in the 80s, the hierarchical structure of the neighborhoods began to change. Young people didn't have the same respect for the elders. It broke down the concept of, "It takes a village to raise a child."

After growing up and seeing the ravages of poor health care and education, as well as drug addiction, I decided it was my duty as Medicine Woman to help my people recover from problems caused by these chronic systemic issues. At the Shrine of the Holy Spirit on Bayou Road, people seek me out for help with health issues and spiritual upliftment—prayers and overall healing.

The significance of the libation is to keep us connected with the earth and to honor the ancestors that have brought us to where we are today. By pouring the libation, I am acknowledging Fi Yi Yi's ancestors, and in the process, my ancestors, too. I am who I am because of all the medicine women and men in me who have healed people before me. We keep our practices alive by repeating what they have taught us.

Kenneth Lewis, wildman of the Mandingo Warriors.

Victor: Kenneth Lewis was my wildman. He was a people's wildman. He had fun with everybody and made people laugh. From the time we were coming up, he loved to follow the Indians and sing. He stayed on the other side of Annette Street from me with his grandmother. His brother, Darryl "Wool" Lewis, was the Nugget Man at our sewing table.

Wesley: He was friends with my family. He would do things for my mother.

Victor: He cut everybody's grass in the neighborhood. He would do good deeds for people, but he'd have them buy him a beer! Believe me! For how crazy he was, he was a very polite person.

Kenneth didn't hide anything he did. He wore a collar and did a lot of preaching while he carried a beer in his hand. They would call him, "Little Loud Preacher Man." I don't care what happened—anything could have happened—he would say, "I'll drink to that!" Some people said he was wrong for that, but I had him bless me. I believe he did because he was honest and sincere. He asked the Lord to help take care of me as his chief.

Top: Shortly after Kenneth was killed, Big Queen Kim Boutte and Al Polit stand with the Spirit of Fi Yi Yi in front of Kenneth Lewis's house before Tambourine & Fan's Super Sunday parade on May 25, 2008. Fi Yi Yi is holding a beer to pour a libation for Kenneth. *Middle:* Al Polit holds Kenneth's wildman staff and a photograph of him during the Super Sunday parade. *Bottom:* Victor Harris with Lionel Delpit, the big chief of the Black Feather, remembering Kenneth. Victor and Lionel came up together in the Yellow Pocahontas before both branching out with their own tribes.

Al Polit: Kenneth was killed in May. It was horrible. We came out of that front-a-town section of the Seventh Ward, and Kenneth came up under me in school. Later in life, we spent a lot of time together because of our commitment to Fi Yi Yi. On Super Sunday, I picked up his staff, and something came over me. Something came down from heaven and it hit me. I don't remember what happened the rest of the day, but I was taken back in time. It started for me with Herbert Jones, my dad who raised me. He had a fruit stand on North Claiborne and Laharpe, and ran the streets with Tootie Montana. Tootie and my daddy were Creole people; they spoke Creole with each other. After Fi Yi Yi started, I used to sew by Coach's apartment or beat the drums with the Mandingo Warriors on Carnival day. I didn't know Coach was planting a seed in me that began to grow after Kenneth died.

Victor Harris dressed as a wildman at Kenneth Lewis's funeral on May 27, 2008. Walking behind him, Al Polit holds Kenneth's wildman staff, and Collins "Coach" Lewis carries his picture.

Victor: Kenneth believed in God. We both knew you got to make contact with the spirits, and you've got to believe in what you're doing. For his funeral, I dressed as a wildman as a tribute to him. I decided, "I'm going to be him." I was wild—wild for my wildman.

Sylvester: At a funeral for a Mardi Gras Indian, other Indians will mask to pay respect for the time the person put into
the culture. It is like a jazz funeral, but with Indian songs.
When Kenny was brought out, we sang, "Indian Red."

Top: Mardi Gras Indians waiting to receive Kenneth's
casket as the pallbearers leave the church. ***Bottom:*** Victor
as wildman leads the pallbearers and mourners during
Kenneth's jazz funeral procession while Sylvester Francis
(*on right*) films.

Claire Tancons, curator of the Spirit of Fi Yi Yi and the Mandingo Warriors' Prospect.1 exhibit at the New Orleans Museum of Art. Originally from Guadeloupe, her exhibits and writing focus on Carnival traditions around the African diaspora. She is the co-author of *En Mas': Carnival and Performance Art in the Caribbean* with Krista A. Thompson.

The Spirit of Fi Yi Yi and the Mandingo Warriors exhibit opening for the Prospect.1 Art Bienalle at the New Orleans Museum of Art.

Ronald Dumas: At the New Orleans Musem of Art, I got up from amongst the audience and made a statement. I told Victor, "I will be your next wildman." Jack and Coach looked at me like I was a damn fool. "We don't know you from nowhere. You come in dressed in a leather jacket looking like Superfly!"

But I felt connected. I'm a genealogist of St. James Parish in Côté des Allemands, the German Coast. When I first moved to New Orleans, I learned about the Backstreet Cultural Museum, and met some of the guys in Fi Yi Yi. Then I went to hear an artist talk they did at the art museum. When I listened to their story, something got ahold of me about how they have returned to their roots. I come from a Creole community called Shell Hill. My grandfather, Henri, cut shares with Antoine Fats Domino's father on the Coteau Plantation.

It is a hard history. After the whip, those people were working for shares with no rights. In the off seasons, my family would get away from the sugar cane plantations and come to New Orleans. It was an escape for a while. As a young kid, I grew up speaking Creole. In the 1960s, they tried to force us to speak English. If they caught us speaking Creole in school, they made us kneel down on rice and hold our hands out with dictionaries. I never understood what was wrong with our language, why we couldn't practice our culture back home.

My life-long goal is able to share a perspective of Creole culture that also respects the indigenous cultures in Louisiana. In the area where I grew up, there are remnants of shell mounds built by indigenous people. In 1856, our Lady of Peace Catholic Church was built where one is located. Local government used those shells with human bones in it to pave the roads. There were no laws to protect the site. Up until this day, many people on the German Coast will not talk about what was there. That's a great disrespect to the ancestors. I thought Fi Yi Yi would understand what I've been trying to talk about.

2 0 0 9

Left: Jack Robertson and Victor Harris working on individual beaded patches that will be sewn onto fabric to create the aprons, mask, and other parts of the Fi Yi Yi suit. **Right:** Perry Emery, flagboy for the Mandingo Warriors, sewing at Victor's house.

Perry Emery, Flagboy of the Mandingo Warriors: I met Vic when I was 15 years old. He was my brother Edward's supervisor at Charity Hospital. Edward was working on the student summer program, and when he graduated from school, they got him on full-time. Vic became a family friend. He co-signed my brother's first car, and he is Edward's first son's godfather.

In the early 1990s, I was in my 20s and working for the Housing Authority of New Orleans as a store-room keeper. I used to come over to Vic's in the evenings to thread needles and take pictures. I was just excited to be around them. I donated material, listened to stories, and the next thing I knew I'm at the table sewing.

Coach showed me how to sew; how the gang go. He argued with Jack like they were a couple. One thing about Coach, he was real religious. You'd catch him singing old-time religious hymns. And one thing I noticed about Vic was that he was always going to make sure the kids had their suits together before he came out. Some times that means everyone is running a little late. In 1993, some of the other guys in the gang went out without him because they didn't want to wait any longer. When Vic came out, he had to meet everyone himself. I could see he was tired. A guy named Charlie and I decided to join the tribe because we liked his priorities. I follow behind him because he's thinking about the kids. He's always looking back. He takes money out of his pocket and does a back to school giveaway in the neighborhood.

I started masking when I was 27. Not everyone in the tribe wears a mask, but I decided I would sew one to complement Vic. I like how we create suits other people don't have to carry. We can wear them all day. When you wear the mask, people don't know who you are. That's okay with me because I like to be known for the beauty of it—playing the game.

Perry Emery masking as flagboy of the Mandingo Warriors.

Perry: I started as spyboy. I went out and scouted. As spyboy, you are the first to meet another tribe. You get to see all the action. If you meet another spyboy who is ready to play Indian, you can have fun dancing and ribbing each other. Then you bring it to the flagboy to let them know who's coming.

Now I am flagboy. In this position, you have more say so. On Carnival day, Chief is in his glory: singing, taking pictures. He's the president; flagboys are secret service. Victor and I are wearing the masks so we can't see as well. I try to keep the route in front of us open; not too crowded with people. I watch him at all times, and I'm looking at Victor's eyes. If he gives me the nod, I know what he wants to do.

The years I haven't masked, Vic has said, "I sure miss my flagboy because he keep people off me." There is a lot going on all the time. People do crazy things when they are drinking and smoking. Some Indians who aren't chiefs want to meet Victor. They'll say, "I want to see my uncle." If they aren't a big chief, they have to take their crown off. Sometimes it gets hard, but you have to be firm because chances are it's not just going to be a hello—the other Indian is going to stand there and try to challenge Victor.

Top left: Victor Harris as the Spirit of Fi Yi Yi with his little queens at Tambourine & Fan's Super Sunday parade. Victor often comes out with a different mask after Carnival for St. Joseph's night and Super Sunday. *Top right:* Big Chief Bruce Sunpie Barnes and Second Chief Zohar Israel of the Northside Skull and Bone Gang parade with Fi Yi Yi down Orleans Avenue during Super Sunday. *Bottom right:* Howard Miller, a childhood friend of Jack Robertson, playing the tambourine with the Creole Wild West's second line at Super Sunday. Howard is the co-big chief of the tribe with Lil Walter Cook.

Victor Harris as the honorary grand marshal of Sudan Social & Pleasure Club's 2009 parade.

Fred Johnson, President of Black Men of Labor Social Aid and Pleasure Club: When we were young, I worked with Victor and Coach to get ready for parades at 2258 North Robertson. We spent a lot of nights in the Building working on streamers, fans, and umbrellas for Tambourine & Fan's second line club, the Bucket Men.

Victor: When the Bucket Men stopped parading, some of the members started Sudan Social and Pleasure Club. Years later, Fred and some of the other members started Black Men of Labor. Sudan, Black Men of Labor, and a lot of members of Yellow Pocahontas and Fi Yi Yi trace their roots back to Tambourine & Fan.

Bernard Robertson, Co-Founder of Sudan Social and Pleasure Club: Since the club's existence in 1983, Sudan has had a formula to honor someone from our community—someone who enlightened us—as the honorary grand marshal of our annual second line parade.

Victor: I started Fi Yi Yi a year later!

Bernard: The first year, we came out of St. Augustine Catholic Church 35 strong. We had brothers from all over. It was a two-hour parade throwing roses. We had some patent leather shoes because we were wearing tuxedos, and it was hot. The ground burned your feet. But we were so proud to come out.

In 2009, David Crowder claimed it was time for Victor Harris to be honored. Now, there are many reasons we could claim, but the main reason would be Victor's loyalty to the children of the community. We could also be biased and say that he was our coach and our shield on Hunter's Field.

Back then, we always gathered to the sound of the bass drum. The older coaches in Tambourine & Fan started it. The kids would be playing and one of the coaches would beat the drum. When we heard the sound, we had to stop what

Left to right: Sudan Social and Pleasure Club members Mario Harris, Bernard Robertson, Adrian Gaddies, and Les Domonique perform a dirge at their annual second line parade.

we were doing and run to it: "When the drum beat, move your feet!" Before and after games, we would beat the drum, too. I have talked to other people who said, "Man, you came to the park with all that noise! Even if you lost a game, you made so much noise everybody thought you'd won!"

Victor: We integrated St. Roch Park. I'm talking about us—nobody one else! We had to take over Barracks Park in the French Quarter. We said to the white folks, "We will play you, but you can't tell us we can't come."

Bernard: Sometimes there would be a jamboree with teams from all over the city, and the playground was so terrible the coaches wouldn't allow the kids to go out there. Jerome Smith would give the order to take them in the middle of the field. Everybody sat in the middle of the field like, "Nobody going to play!" We demonstrated, and Victor and the other coaches protected us.

Coach Collins and Gerald Emile came up with songs. Coach had so many, but some of them were freedom songs. And the one that always had me was:

If my mother don't go...

Victor: *If my mother don't go,*

Bernard: *I'm going to journey right on.*

Victor: *I'm going to journey right on.*

Bernard: *Well, if my mother don't go!*

Victor: *I'm going to journey right on....*

Bernard: *I've done signed up! Made up my mind!*

Victor: At parades, one of the things I always noticed was that Bernard was a banner carrier.

Bernard: We were raised to be proud to represent whoever we were. When we were kids, Victor was running with the Yellow Pocahontas. We would go to different parts of the city, and on the way back the Indians would be tired: "Vic! Vic! Let me hold your crown!" Vic would gladly let you hold his crown. Now, going uptown? No, because he had to meet everybody. But coming back down, the meeting is over, and everyone was tired. I learned you couldn't let the crown drag, you had to hold it with your hands in the air, and that's how I picked up carrying something.

For the parade in 2009, we told Vic, "We got a car for you." Victor was our first honorary grand marshal who didn't want a car. I believe he walked the whole parade.

Victor: I walked with my drummers behind me. I didn't want to ride in a car like a senator waving my hand.

Bernard: The Spirit walked the whole parade. That was a shocker for us. He wanted to be with the people. Not above the people, but in the crowd with the people.

Fred: It was our honor to receive Sudan and Victor as their grand marshal. It was like a homecoming.

Top: Todd Higgins raises his fist as Victor Harris meets Black Men of Labor Social Aid and Pleasure Club at Sweet Lorraine's Jazz Club on St. Claude Avenue. Black Men of Labor hosted a stop for Sudan's parade. Designer Melvin Reed is standing on the right side of the photograph in a checkered brown shirt.
Bottom: Co-founder of Sudan, Adrian "Coach Teedy" Gaddies (*with hands up*), dances to the New Birth Brass Band.

David Crowder, co-founder of Sudan Social and Pleasure Club, wearing a streamer he created for their annual second line parade.

Bernard: Whoever reads this book, they have a spirit. A spirit is in everyone. Do you bring that spirit out and let it shine? Some people do. For some reason, when we were growing up, Tambourine & Fan brought it out. Victor got it, took it to another level, and left enough for us to follow behind.

I will never be a Fi Yi Yi, but I am Bernard of Sudan with the spirit that Fi Yi Yi has. And that goes for Adrian Gaddies, David Crowder, John Dobar, Archie Chapman, and the deceased Kenneth Dykes. That goes for the kids who played ball, which could be ten thousand. Later, I became a coach. Even when I got in trouble, I never left the kids because of what I saw in Fi Yi Yi's eyes. When he put his hands around me, I was mesmerized with his love of the children.

2 0 1 0

·•·•·

Victor Harris putting on face paint at Wesley Phillips's house in the Seventh Ward on Carnival day. He is surrounded by Mandingo Warriors' outfits on display.

Victor: As the Spirit of Fi Yi Yi, I have to make my tribe rise. As we are getting ready, I don't want them to see me. I close myself off and go in the mirror. I start putting my paint on and I'm going into deep thought. I go into a trance. When I come out of the room, I'm where I want to be. They are looking in my eyes. They are going, "Chief ready now." I don't say anything and then, prepare yourself now: "Ahhhhhh!!!"

I go to screaming. Boy, it looks like everybody's jumping out the door. Those are some of the most exciting times in my life. I'm in their faces. I'm making them become one with the spirit. I start with their eyes and it goes into their hearts.

Big Queen Cutie, Kim Boutte, putting on face paint at Wesley Phillips's house in the Seventh Ward.

Kim: Whenever we paint our faces, I write "R.I.P. Matt-Matt." My son, Matthew, was a sportsman. I named him after my brother, who was killed in the Florida Project over dope. My son was killed after Katrina; the day before Mother's day in the Eighth Ward. He was only 15 years old. He had woken up early to go shopping for his school clothes. Some boys robbed him, and they shot him.

I've lost a lot of family from violence over drugs. My other brother, my cousins. I visit my son almost every other day at the Providence Cemetery. He is buried by my brother and grandparents. I wear a necklace around my neck with his picture. I never take it off except to go to bed.

Sylvester Francis, Jr. on Carnival morning at the Backstreet, where he deejays for the large crowds that gather and announces the different organizations who arrive to pay tribute to the museum.

Sylvester Francis, Jr.: I've stuck with my daddy from a kid. He has 12 children and we all stayed close to him. I am the oldest. My daddy taught me about the culture, being a man out here, and believing in yourself. When I turned 13 years old, he bought my first stereo set, and I deejayed my own birthday party. Hanging with him and Mardi Gras Indians, I picked up different styles of music and went from there. The museum is his pride and joy. When he decided he needed help, I was there with him. I do a little bit of everything. You don't have just one title.

Second Chief Zohar Israel with young members of the Northside Skull and Bone Gang visit trumpeter Kermit Ruffins's bar, Sidney's Saloon, in the Seventh Ward early on Carnival morning. Zohar is the founder of the Free Spirit African Drum and Dance Company. His son, Shaka Zulu, masks with the Yellow Pocahontas.

Zohar Israel, Second Chief of the Northside Skull and Bone Gang: The Northside comes to warn you that you've got to straighten up your life. You've got to change your life. You know Yahweh says we have to be moral, righteous, upright, honest, and responsible. We have to take care of our children. We have to know not to put bad things in our bodies; we have to protect our temple. These are the things we warn people about. Do not to take advantage of children. You participate in things like trafficking children, it's going to

catch up with you, and you're going to have to come and see us. The bone gang.

The stilts are a tall spirit. It's still the bone man, just a tall one. The stilts became very popular, and lots of photographs have been taken. I'm basically the overseer. I go out in the front of the gang, see what's coming, and keep the gang alert. I lead the direction the crowd is going to go, and stop traffic.

Victor: Besides official stops, if I see a person who seems interested in the suit, I'm going to go over to them and interact with them because they are out there for a reason, too. I like to get close to them, touch them, and be in their faces. They never expect personally to encounter that: it gives them something to talk about.

Victor Harris as the Spirit of Fi Yi Yi greeting neighbors in the Seventh Ward on Carnival day.

Top: The Spirit of Fi Yi Yi and the Mandingo Warriors visiting Kermit Ruffins's Sidney's Saloon on St. Bernard Avenue on St. Joseph's night.
Bottom: Wesley Phillips drumming under I-10 on North Claiborne Avenue.

Wesley: On St. Joseph's night, Fi Yi Yi came by my house on North Claiborne to get ready, but it was a bad time for me. My brother, Byron Phillips, had just died unexpectedly. There were all these people getting ready, and I had to leave to make the program for Byron's funeral the next day. When I came back, I joined my tribe. I wasn't planning on playing at the funeral because I thought I would be too emotional, but playing the djembe under the bridge on Claiborne gave me a chance to play for my little brother's spirit. My heart was heavy. The sound of the drums hitting on the concrete created a full sound that felt like a big relief. It was my own private contribution to his send-off.

Kim: We have kids with us and they be small. They like it out there. When we come out, we stay in the neighborhood because of them. We sit under the bridge and start rolling out there. I teach my little girls to dance. They have their swords in their hands and I say, "Open it up, baby! Are you going to be little queen or what?" They used to be crying, but now they like it. When they watch me, they catch on, and start rolling with me. I tell them, "I'm going to go get them like you go get 'em."

Victor: On the street, the girls are more warriors than the boys. When there's trouble, they won't run. And they all watch Kim. She's taught them how to dance, and how to stand up for themselves.

Kim: We call my niece Makira "Big Coodie." She says she's too big now. She told me, "I want new clothes for Mardi Gras." I asked her, "A new Indian suit doesn't count?" She texted me later, "Teedy, don't be mad I don't want to be an Indian no more."

I said, "I'm not mad. I'll recruit some more girls."

Makira "Big Coodie" Boutte dancing with her aunt, Big Queen Cutie, Kim Boutte, under the I-10 overpass on North Claiborne.

2 0 1 1

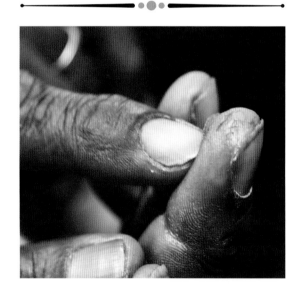

Portrait of Jack Robertson with a beaded staff in front of a backdrop of marabou.

Dijonaise Harris's son, Adrian, watches his grandfather as the Spirit of Fi Yi Yi before the tribe meets the Yellow Pocahontas under the bridge on North Claiborne Avenue.

Shaka Zulu: I knew Victor before I knew he was Fi Yi Yi because he worked with my uncle at Charity Hospital, but I didn't make the connection to Fi Yi Yi. On the street, he never took the mask off.

I grew up with my father, Zohar Israel's, Free Spirit African Drum Company. We are stilt dancers and often wear full masks. I've been initated into a lot of masking societies in Africa. When you put a mask on, you are not a person anymore. You become the energy of the entity of what you are masking. There is a lot you go through when you design a suit. When you put it on, you are connecting with the emotions you went through. You can feel the power of the spirit when people don't know who you are.

This year, the big chief of the Yellow Pocahontas, Darryl Montana, didn't come out, so I had to carry the tribe. I created the Shango suit after the Yoruba orisha. We usually have a lot of tambourines, but I decided to include more African drums. When we met Fi Yi Yi, you could feel the adrenaline spike to encounter another mask. The African soundtrack took me back to when I was a little boy. Fi Yi Yi's drummer, Wesley Phillips, was raised in the Desire Projects where I grew up. He was my drum teacher when I was five years old in the Teach Your Brother program. When we met, I don't think either one of us wanted to say too much to take away from that energy, but Fi Yi Yi said, "Boy, you pretty."

Shaka Zulu, wearing his Shango suit, prepares to meet the Spirit of Fi Yi Yi.

Jackie Alford, Big Queen of Black Feather:
On St. Joseph's night, Black Feather met Fi Yi Yi on St. Bernard Avenue. I love to see Kim and the girls. We grew up together and we're like family. We played baseball together. As a queen, she don't dress heavy because she likes to dance.

Kim: Jackie's my girl. She can sew, but I told her, "You can't just walk and be pretty." When we go to Indian practice, I show her how to dance.

Jackie: Fi Yi Yi is the main person we look forward to meeting. When you look at his mask and see Fi Yi Yi's eyes, he's going to let you know that you sewed your suit. Your suit was ready! He's going to give you that respect. Lionel had spirit in him, too. I used to be scared to be masking, but when he started singing, it didn't matter how heavy my suit was, I felt light.

This was his last year that Lionel masked. I never thought it would have been the last time I would wear a suit for my chief. We were by his side when he died. I said, "Don't leave me, Chief." Afterwards, it felt like we were Broken Feather. I'm waiting for the spirit to tell me it's all right to mask again. When I do, I'm going to be a monster. They ain't going to be ready.

Victor: I didn't know that this was the last season that Coach and I were going to be together either. It wasn't in my mind at all.

Top: Big Queen of the Black Feather, Jackie Alford, meeting Big Queen Cutie, Kim Boutte, on St. Joseph's night. *Bottom:* Victor Harris meeting Big Chief Lionel Delpit of Black Feather.

Sunpie: Coach was a great gospel singer with a resounding voice. He knew how to do shape note singing, and created harmonies. He loved to voice his opinion, but he wanted you to voice your own, which is why it made sense he connected with African drumming.

Cinnamon Black: Coach told me, "Where I grew up ain't there no more. I grew up near Congo Square, which is now called Louis Armstrong Park. Now it's everyone's home." Coach liked to go to Congo Square on Sundays to join the drummers who still gather there to play African rhythms. He'd tell me, "Somebody got to show up here on Sunday because of the grandfather clause." He believed if we ever stopped, we may have to start applying for a city permit to play music there.

Every July, we gathered for Maafa to remember the black holocaust of the Middle Passage where Africans were captured and taken across the Atlantic to be enslaved. We wear white. We release birds in memory of the enslaved who died and have a healing service with libations. As the procession leaves Congo Square, we stand at the gateway to pray to take the spirits of the ancestors to the Mississippi River to set their souls free.

Maafa is a Kiswahili word that means "great tragedy" or "horrific tragedy." In 2000, Douglas Redd and Carol Bebelle, co-founders of the Ashé Cultural Center, worked with Leia Lewis to start the first commemoration of the Middle Passage in New Orleans. They were inspired by St. John the Baptist Church's programs around Maafa in Brooklyn, New York. *Top left:* Coach sings at the beginning of the Maafa ceremony at Congo Square. Originally Choctaw land, the area became part of the City Commons during the colonial era, and was claimed by enslaved Africans during the 1800s for a market on Sundays. The gatherings became legendary for their music and dancing, and are said to be one of the reasons why New Orleans has retained a strong connection to its African heritage. In the 1970s, many blocks of the Tremé neighborhood, where Coach grew up, were torn down to build a "Cultural Center." Both are now part of Louis Armstrong Park. *Top and bottom right:* Libations are poured and members of the procession are cleansed with sage as they begin their procession to the Mississippi River.

Top: Victor Harris as the Spirit of Fi Yi Yi during the procession from Congo Square during Maafa. ***Right:*** Cinnamon Black kneeling at the Tomb for the Unknown Slave while wearing the beaded collar she made with Collins "Coach" Lewis in 2008.

Cinnamon Black: During the Maafa procession, we lay flowers at the Tomb of the Unknown Slave in front of St. Augustine Catholic Church before going to the river.

Kim: The last time I was with Coach, we were walking on a Sunday to the second line across the Canal and his feet looked swollen. He said "Yeah, they swoll, but we going anyway."

Victor: The last time I saw him, we were getting ready for an event in Congo Square. He told me, "It's going to be hot out there with all your stuff on. You got to take care of yourself. Make sure you be all right." He said, "I'm going home, me. I'll see you tomorrow." He was so kind in the way he was talking. He was being polite to people.

Jack: Coach fed everybody in his new apartment building and everything.

Victor: Nice to everybody! We said, "What is going on?" When I got the news that he died, those words he was saying opened my eyes. Man, he was telling me he was going home.

We have some films of Coach and sometimes it makes me feel good just to hear him. Just like he is there for me. His voice be so clear. His voice is more clear to me now because he is not around. I am listening more than I ever listened to him before.

Cinnamon Black: Every day after he died, Coach's commitment to protecting this land haunted me. He was telling me to remember the land, remember the dirt. I think he is a part of Congo Square. I think he is a part of us.

Victor Harris at a drum circle in front of the Backstreet Cultural Museum that was organized in honor of Collins "Coach" Lewis in the days leading up to his funeral.

Perry: You go to a person's funeral, it can tell you about the type of person they were.

Ausettua: Coach was a person who loved peace and camaraderie amongst men. He had the power to unify them.

Victor: Coach was blessed with a royal service. He was sent out the right way. The spirit in Charbonnet Funeral Home was awesome. Truly, it was. A lot of well-known people have funeral services where official people speak without knowledge of the culture, but at Coach's service, he had the people of the culture he loved. It was the greatest service I have ever been to. He belonged to the culture and the culture was there for him.

Ausettua: When we have to bury someone close to us, it's always surreal. In West Africa, ancestors are part of the living community. For Coach, we danced a dance the Yoruba people of Nigeria perform when they approach a shrine to the ancestors.

Reverend Goat Carson led an opening prayer at Collins "Coach" Lewis's service and asked children to come up and choose a beaded patch to remember him by.

Janet Sula Evans: I am the Founding Priestess of the Temple of Light, Ile de Coin-Coin, located in New Orleans' Musician's Village. I knew Coach for more than 15 years and was honored to perform burial rites on his body with Andaiye Alimayu when he transitioned into the ancestral realm. During the burial rites, the deceased's body is smoked with frankincense and myrrh and marked with sacred oils. Burial rites are a symbol of honor and respect for the life he lived, and is a way we give reverence to the sacred energy that was embodied in the form of Coach. While performing the rites, the dominant spirit I felt from him was gratitude.

Sunpie: One night the great Nigerian drummer, Ayan Bisi Adeleke, was at St. Augustine Church, and we all played talking drums. Coach said, "You see this. This is real for me. This is what I would like at my funeral. When I go, you've got to bring those African drums." I was proud to be able to meet his request.

Wesley: We also played the *Lamba* rhythm from Mali as Jamila Peters-Muhammed performed the dance of royalty for Coach.

Top: Janet Sula Evans and Andaiye Alimayu perform burial rites for Collins "Coach" Lewis. ***Bottom:*** In the forefront, Ricky Gettridge, Wesley Phillips, Luther Grey, and Bruce Sunpie Barnes drum in honor of Coach while Jamila Peters-Muhammed and Ausettua Amor Amenkum Jackson lead a dance of royalty.

Both pages: Al Polit, Wesley Phillips, and Jack Robertson perform a
mourning ceremony for Collins "Coach" Lewis with Victor Harris as the
Spirit of FiYiYi at Charbonnet Funeral Home in Tremé.

Al: Coach wasn't just there for me for the Indian time,
Coach was there for me for my whole life. He used to stay
by himself, and when he was going through his life storm,
he came with me. I had a floor covering business and he
became my right hand man. Coach helped build my house
and other people's houses, too. He helped a lot of people.

Victor: He was my everything. He brought everything to the table and he didn't make no excuses.

Fred Johnson: Coach was a right and left hand to Victor. He was a serious link in the chain for all of us. His death made me understand that we are all on this timeline. None of us are going to get out of here alive, but we never know when the timeline will end. Seeing him in that casket brought the reality of life in front of me. I talked to Coach's sister, Janice, and said Black Men of Labor Social Aid and Pleasure Club would be the pall bearers. We brought him out of Charbonnet Funeral Home and the musicians were waiting for him.

Top: Fred Johson and Todd Higgins from Black Men of Labor Social Aid and Pleasure Club bring the casket of Collins "Coach" Lewis out of Charbonnet Funeral Home. ***Bottom:*** Trombonist Percy Anderson, trumpeter Kermit Ruffins, and bass drummer Michael Duffy gather for Coach's jazz funeral procession outside of Charbonnet.

Collins "Coach" Lewis's jazz funeral in Tremé.

Sylvester: I danced one dance for Coach. That's all I could do. I wasn't ready.

Cinnamon Black: It was very hard to say goodbye to Coach, but I know that his spirit will always be alive through what we do. He would say, "We didn't get nobody to make it for us. We were creative with our minds and our hands. We slept it, walked it, talked it." He always would say, "This is how we did it."

2 0 1 2

125

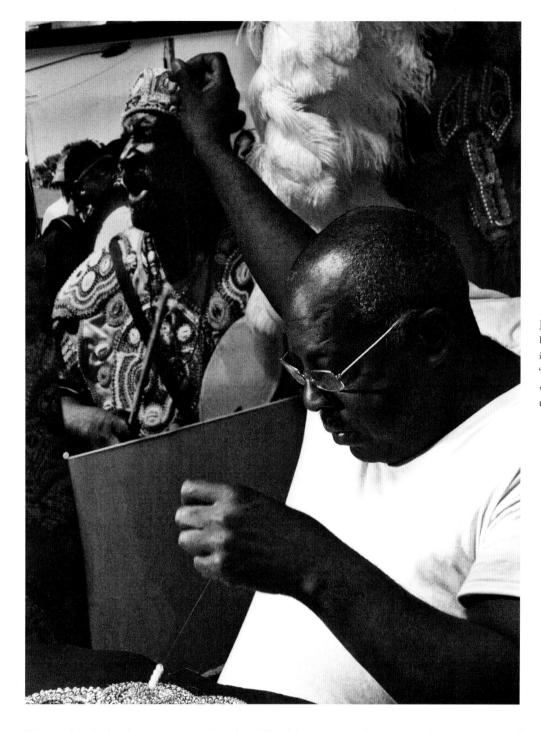

Jack sewing the
Bumpy Blue suit
in honor of Collins
"Coach" Lewis
with a picture of
Coach next to him.

Victor: Mr. Jack is the last one at the table. The others are dead. It has been hard for me to sit here and all of these people who have been with me from the beginning of time are no longer around me. Sammy Graham and Alvin Landry. Sam Griffin who would do the hook up and wires. And now Coach. Sometimes Jack and I be in here and he says, "Man, it's just you and me." And I say, "Yeah, but we got to do better than we've been doing."

Jeffrey: I don't want to start crying and I don't want to get too mushy, but I loved Coach, who was an impossible human being and absolutely...

Victor: Without him, it wasn't too much the life of the party. Without him being there, you don't hear nobody talking. He's the one who always brought it out. He had a habit of spilling the beads. He'd close his eyes and listen to the sound of the beads go through his hands. You'd hear that little sound and next thing you know everything was on the floor. A thousand times he did it. Any time one of us does it now, I say, "That's Coach. He's here." We created the "Bumpy Blue" suit for him because that was one of his nicknames.

Ronald Dumas as the Mandingo Warrior's wildman peers
out of Wesley Phillips's house on Carnival morning.

Ronald: After I started following Fi Yi Yi, I thought
I could go in their den at Drummer's house. But I was wrong.
Drummer wouldn't let me in his house. I had to sit on the
curb and wait for them to come out on Carnival day.

In 2012, Sylvester helped put me on the streets of New
Orleans. I didn't know how to sew. He said, "Your color is
bumpy blue." We went to Walgreens and got a blue sheet.
I covered it in moss, deer antlers, coon tails, and work boots.
I wanted to evoke the swamp, our safe haven. To me, the
wildman stands for the winter: from All Saints' day until the
Twelfth House of Pisces. The dark cycle. When I became the
wildman, I was finally let into Drummer's house. I felt like
I done made it. Still, everyone was skeptical.

Al: When Chief said, "We got a new wildman." I said,
"Who this is? Kenneth Lewis was our wildman." I went to
Ronald and crashed horns with him. I nearly tried to knock
him down.

Ronald: But I can't be Kenny. We are two different persons.
Kenneth had been a minister. I am a minister, too. My pastor
told me just like my chief: "When you get up to get a ceremony, you need your power. You get your power from God."
I had to follow their routes to learn how they earned respect.

Victor: It's knowing how to communicate. The people
who come out to see me know I'm an honorable person. My
mother said, "Be yourself, and you'll be surprised what you
can do." You can make a person well. You can heal these
people with the goodness in your heart. I don't even try to
be special. I get out a lot out of being a servant, rather than
be served.

Left: Victor Harris as the Spirit of Fi Yi Yi stops traffic on North Claiborne Avenue. ***Top right***: Victor sitting down at the stop Ms. Ruby Pipkins's family hosts for Fi Yi Yi on Carnival day in the Seventh Ward. ***Bottom right:*** The Spirit of Fi Yi Yi meeting neighborhood children in the Seventh Ward.

Jack: The Pipkins family hosts a stop for us every year on Touro Street in the Seventh Ward. Ms.Ruby likes us to come by the house. She's up in age now.

Louis Pipkins: This is what we like to do. The house on Touro was my grandfather's house. My father bought it from him in the late 1950s right after he had us. My mama, Ruby, had 10 children so we had a crowd ourselves. The house has a good spirit to it. A few years ago, my brother and I moved back in. All the grandchildren gather here. They say this area is like the French Quarters now. It's mostly whites who are moving in, but they're good neighbors. Everybody's music a little loud. Second line bands still come through.

Victor: Indians used to have stops at people's houses, and they would have food for you. There would be stops all through the neighborhood, but the Pipkins are the only stop now that has food for all of us.

Louis: This rest stop is a tradition. Vic has been a friend all of our lives. When we were young, we used to sew by his house and followed him on Carnival. Now everybody in the neighborhood, black and white, waits for him here because they know he is coming around. And we really appreciate him coming. Even though we are all spread out around the city, we come together for Carnival. When Victor gets everyone ready to make that last run, I'll clean up and walk with them.

Victor: When we are walking around and I see kids on the street, I mess with them. If some of them are scared, sometimes I run after them just to play with them; make them run. It reminds me of when my own kids were small. My son, Lil Vic, started with me the first year I masked as Fi Yi Yi in 1984. He was four years old. He looked out the door at all them people and ran back inside. He grabbed me by the leg and told me, "I ain't going out there, Dad, without you." Once we came out together, he was running around jumping all over the place. I still enjoy the wonder.

Perry: You can see it on the kids' faces. You'll be surprised how much they know about the culture. When I worked for the Housing Authority, I used to go into the projects and kids would say, "That's Fi Yi Yi!" The parents would say, "You don't know what you're talking about," and I'd have to correct them, "Actually, I do mask." They remember.

The Spirit of Fi Yi Yi walking with Voodoo Baby Doll Second Queen Resa "Cinnamon Black" Bazile and Big Queen Cutie, Kim Boutte, during the Mardi Gras Indian Council's Super Sunday parade.

Cinnamon Black: I costume all the time. I've worked at the Voodoo Historical Museum in the French Quarter as the character of Marie Laveau since 1980, and do a lot of acting.

Victor: Cinnamon is a real Marie Laveau—I see it in her eyes. That's where you look.

Cinnamon Black: I've been a baby doll since 1974. I liked following Fi Yi Yi with Coach, but after he died, I didn't know if I was in all the way with the whole tribe.

Perry: At first it was like, "Cinnamon is Coach's friend."

Kim: When I first met her, she asked me how she can join our group. I said, "You can be the baby doll but you can't be the big queen. Ain't none of them go over me."

Cinnamon Black: Victor finally gave me a title in the tribe. He said, "You be who you are: You are a Voodoo Baby Doll Queen." These Indians was unlike any other group I have been with—the engaging in ideas, the costuming, the expressions. The language is outspoken, but it comes from a feeling inside your heart.

Victor: Cinnamon learned quickly. She has good eyes and can really sew. She came to the right camp, and she was taught well. She does all her own.

Cinnamon Black: Kim has been the big queen for many years. Understanding my role as second queen is a learning experience. I have to protect her but not overstep her. I have to follow her around. I have to be by her side. I have two responsibilities because everything is supportive of both the chief and the queen. Kim and I are like night and day. I know it takes a long time to get respected from another queen. I have to watch her more than she watches me. It's a line of order.

Kim: She's got to follow my footsteps. She got to really learn the Indian steps. We've gotten closer and closer.

Cinnamon Black: With my stage background and Kim's street movements, we marry together.

After leaning back all the way to the ground, Victor Harris as the Spirit of Fi Yi Yi lays in A.L. Davis (Shakespeare) Park at the end of the Mardi Gras Indian Council's Super Sunday parade while Al Polit plays a cowbell and Wildman Ronald Dumas continues his quest for power.

Ronald: The first year I masked as wildman, Victor had me on a chain. He wouldn't let me go very far and I didn't know why. We're a tribe and we do things together, but everyone goes on their own journey when they mask as well. I had a lot to learn because I didn't understand everything going on around me.

Al: At the end of the parade, Chief was worshiping. When Kenneth died, he did a ceremony in the Seventh Ward for

him where he leaned all the way back to the ground, and lay there. He did the same thing for Coach at the end of the Super Sunday parade.

Ronald: I didn't know what he was doing, that he was grieving Coach. When Victor was on the ground, I was trying to pull power from him. I didn't know it was like I was pulling power from the grave.

2 0 1 3

134

Mandingo Warriors's spyboy, Al Polit, wearing his suit dedicated to Collins "Coach" Lewis.

Al: I asked Victor, "Chief, can I run as spy?" He said, "Yes, but give me five years." I decided I wanted to make a suit for Coach. Chief and Jack helped me. Wesley gave me the concept of the color. He told me, "You need to pull that color out." White was the color of heaven. The gold beads were the streets paved in gold. Coach was up in the cloud with his tambourine.

Opposite Page: Victor Harris as the Spirit of Fi Yi Yi coming out of the house next to the Backstreet Cultural Museum on Carnival day. *Top:* Spyboy Al Polit walking through some of the coldest and wettest Carnival weather on record. *Bottom:* Folk artist Ashton Ramsey wearing his suit "Menu."

Al: My first year, it was cold and drizzling rain, and I had my two brothers, Stanley Jones and Johnny McLaughlin, carrying the plastic for me. I was going to get my chief. I remember Spyboy Fred Johnson singing a song years ago when I followed the Yellow Pocahontas:

Drizzling rain,
I got the whole goddamn gang
dripping down my neck.
The only thing that made them mad,
they wish they had the gang we had.

Even though the weather was bad, all day I was overcome with the love and the attention people were giving me. They were saying so much good stuff about Coach. It was like Coach was walking with me. All the females were crying, tears dripping from their eyes. Even the men gave me dap and said how much they loved the suit. The other Indians came to me, "Beautiful suit, bra." I opened up, but instead of showing off, they reached out and shook my hand.

Ashton: This suit I made is called "Menu." Survival food: chitlins, kidney stew, court bouillon (fish head without the eyes and teeth), chicken feet, rabbit, pigeon. Blackened redfish was a delicacy for us. I like to go over by the Backstreet to share it because you get to see a lot of people. It is a place where you get to meet Indians, skeletons, baby dolls, and everyday people who come just to see what's going on. The people in Fi Yi Yi and the Mandingo Warriors has changed over time, but I still know a lot of them. Polit was friends with my daughters. They were bummers together.

Ronald: Leading up to Carnival, I met Al Morris, the big chief of the Northside Skull and Bone Gang. He said a wildman needed horns and told me, "I got a set I'll give you." He gave me the horns on Sylvester's steps of the Backstreet.

On Mardi Gras day, we were on our way to pay tribute to Tootie and Joyce Montana. There were quite a few Indians out on the street that day. Victor told me not to go out too far, but when we got to Ms. Joyce's house, I crossed into an area I shouldn't have been in. I wasn't doing it for malice, but ignorance. Another member of the Yellow Pocahontas took precautionary measures. I fell back and grabbed the horns to keep them from falling on the ground. Our big queen, Kim, came up from the front and explained to the Yellow Pocahontas, "He new to the streets." I thought I had power from the Northside Skull and Gang, but I had to reassess.

On Super Sunday, I came out with a different energy. I hadn't met any other wildmen until I met Jaime "Loco" Cooper. I pay great respect to him because he's been around much longer than me. He said, "You look good. You got it." He spun around in his wheelchair and I spun around on the street. That was a joyful moment and it gave me confidence again to join the fraternity of wildmen. I retired the cow horns and haven't worn them since.

Top: Fi Yi Yi and the Yellow Pocahontas meeting in front of Joyce and Tootie Montana's house in the Seventh Ward on Carnival moring. Fi Yi Yi's big queen, Kim Boutte, is standing between Big Chief Darryl Montana of the Yellow Pocahontas and his wife, Sabrina Montana. ***Bottom:*** At the Mardi Gras Indian Council's Super Sunday parade, Wildman Ronald Dumas meets Wildman Jaime "Loco" Cooper.

Victor Harris, Jr., Victor Harris, Kim Boutte, and Al Polit at the Mardi Gras Indian Council's Super Sunday parade.

Victor Jr.: I usually hold off singing until my daddy is ready for me. Then he'll say, "Lil Victor, we need a song! We are going to come together to unite!" We've got to give what the big chief orders. Big Chief gives an order, that's what it is. A rush comes with it.

2 0 1 4

Victor: In 1984, I began Fi Yi Yi wearing black. Every ten
years since then, we have made a black suit. In 2014, I was
making my fourth black suit. I thought, "Time is getting
up there."

Wildman Ronald Dumas meets a masked Indian on Carnival day.

Ronald: As I've masked more, I've started to understand about the power I'd been looking for. You have to pray for your religion. You have to go through trials. In the early 1990s, I was the last generation to be baptized during the Lenten season. It was a symbol of rebirth; to be reborn into the spirit. But it wasn't until I came to New Orleans, this ceremonial center, that I was able to practice my culture.

The Alligator suit was conceived in my mind as a way to go back to the culture of Shell Hill. I was on Lake Allemands, when the idea came to me. I did the tanning and cleaning of the alligator myself. It really pays tribute to my community, and the colors matched Fi Yi Yi's anniversary.

When Mardi Gras Indians talk about remembering runaway slaves, I remember Juan San Malo, the maroon leader who was born near the lake. We had a big cypress lumber industry and runaway slaves lived in the swamps. When I was growing up, the descendents of these maroons still worked in the lumber industry. I learned about it from my ancestor,

Eugene Dumas. *Les gran blancs* (the big whites) tried to reduce our status, but Eugene had San Malo's spirit of rebellion. Years later, his son set the swamp on fire in the fight for better conditions in the lumber industry.

When I wore the suit, I decided I would dedicate all my efforts, all my work and thoughts in my preparation for Carnival, to the ancients that left the mark on the people of Vacherie—both those light and dark in hue—because we are all one. I want to remember the last of the ancient ones like Mr. Moses who lived in the woodlands by the lake. I want to remember the people who left the trout lines. I want to remember the people who understood the harmony of the seasons. I want to hold onto traditions like planting seeds on Good Friday, a very fertile day for our gardens. I would like also to go down as contributing to *la pierre*. It is an acorn from a live oak tree that was found in the lining of a deer. The Indians gave this healing stone to one family from our area, but I believe it should be for all. It is for the healing of the blood.

Top: Big Chief Victor Harris meets Big Chief David Montana of the Washitaw Nation on St. Joseph's night on North Claiborne Avenue. *Middle:* Big Chief Kevin Goodman of the Flaming Arrows stops working on his crown when a crowd rushes into Kermit Ruffins' Mother-in-Law Lounge on St. Joseph's night. *Bottom:* Big Chief Kevin Goodman sings to the big chief of Black Feather, Corey Rayford (*not pictured*). Each moment is documented by photographers who follow different tribes.

Kevin Goodman, Big Chief of Flaming Arrows: Victor has one of the most feared tribes. A lot of Indians don't want to meet them because they seem wild. Victor himself can be scary.

David Montana, Big Chief of the Washitaw Nation: To me, when they sing their song "Fi Yi Yi," it means "Fire on the street." Be careful how you deal with it because you might get burned.

Kevin: I've known Victor from bars in the Sixth Ward like the Tremé Lounge and the Caldonia. We were the first ones to donate suits to the Backstreet, and we've been in a lot of events together by the museum. Even though he's a humble guy, with the Indian suit on he really transforms.

On St. Joseph's night, I still had a couple of things to do with my crown. I call it my hat. We were coming out at Kermit's Mother-in-Law's Lounge on North Claiborne. As we were trying to get everything together, somebody opened the gate and that was it! All these Indians bum-rushed the yard! Victor was one of the first ones to come in and Black Feather was there, too. I wasn't sure what was going on. Corey Rayford, who took over as big chief of Black Feather after Lionel Delpit died, started calling, "I'm coming to see the big chief of Flaming Arrow! That's my big brother! I've got love for him!"

I had to handle my business: "Big Chief ain't ready but we can still play Indian." I was singing, "Somebody got to sew, sew, sew." I knew my suit was pretty, and the other ones coming into the yard would really have had to sew to beat it. Corey and Victor were real pretty, too.

Fi Yi Yi has so many years of experience, but he came to see a younger big chief hit the street. I danced with him for a while. We shook hands and gave each other the peace sign for St. Joseph's night.

Top left: During the Mardi Gras Indian Council's Uptown Super Sunday parade, Big Chief Victor Harris and Flagboy Perry Emery consult on the corner of Washington and LaSalle in Central City, one of the great epicenters of Carnival culture in New Orleans. *Top right:* Victor Harris as the Spirit of Fi Yi Yi looks at his new second spyboy, Keith Polit. *Bottom:* The Spirit of Fi Yi Yi and the Mandingo Warriors parading through Central City.

Keith Polit: I was raised in St. Bernard Parish but grew up coming to New Orleans during Carnival. When my uncle Al started masking spyboy with the Mandingo Warriors, I wanted to know what it was about.

Al: I told him stories about Carnival and Super Sunday and Keith asked, "It really go down like that?" He wanted to join the tribe. He brought Chief a bottle of wine, and asked if he could start sewing. He's been faithful so far as second spy.

Keith: Victor didn't know me, but he opened his arms to me. I had just lost my parents five months apart. On the apron of my first suit, I have the dates of my parents passing. I wished they were here to see me to do it.

Al: Fi Yi Yi and the Mandingo Warriors are a different kind of family. Keith loves it so much his wife started coming out, and his son is talking about how he wants to come with us, too.

Victor Harris and Al Polit visit Hunter's Field where Jerome Smith created an installation to protest violence in New Orleans.

Al: Jerome Smith stopped organizing Downtown Super Sunday. We would wait for the day of the parade to be scheduled, but the months would pass and it wouldn't happen. Jerome said he wanted to do something different to raise awareness about the violence going on in our communities. He put out all of these crosses in Hunter's Field.

Like a lot of people in the Seventh Ward, I was raised there. After I did my homework, my mama would let me go over to play football and run track. With Jerome Smith and all his colleagues, I learned everything about saying no to dope. It kept me off the street, but sometimes we couldn't keep the violence away. We lost a coach while he was practicing with the young boys. A guy got killed during Super Sunday on the field, too. Chief and I stood with Jerome to show our support: Stop the killing.

The Sudan Social and Pleasure Club announces that Sylvester will be their honorary grand marshal at the Backstreet Cultural Museum before the Louis Armstrong parade in August. *Left to right:* Kenneth "Dice" Dykes, Bernard Robertson, Sylvester Francis, and Wendell Carter. Bernard explained to Geraldine Wyckoff, a long time Backstreet supporter and writer for *Offbeat Magazine*: "It goes back to when Sylvester was a young man and he tried to help some kids such as myself to become a man. He had a car wash on St. Bernard and St. Claude, and after we would leave playing football at Hunter's Field, we would go by Sylvester's car wash. We would ask him to buy us a little frozen cup or a sandwich or something. And out of his pocket, he would buy them but at the same time he would tell you, 'Man, you know what, you need to get you a little job. I'm looking for a little alligator.' He was trying to teach the kids that you have to work for what you want. Later, he'd let kids hold his camera and talk to you about photography."

Kendrick Johnson and Bernard Robertson parading with Sudan at the start of the Satchmo SummerFest parade in August. Kendrick holds the "Chinese House" that he worked on with master designers Adrian "Coach Teedy" Gaddies and David Crowder.

Bernard: I'm a second liner. Some people may say, "He can't dance," but I'm an entertainer. When I hear that bass drum, and the drummer is really getting with it, I will wiggle, wiggle, wiggle, and try to make a woman say, "Ooohhhh!"

I asked Melvin Reed to make me a violin, and I became the fiddler of peace. When people came up to me while the brass band music was playing, I asked them if they could hear the violin: "You heard it? You got to listen deep! It's going to come to you."

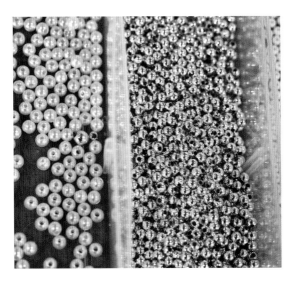

2 0 1 5

Above: Victor, Jr. begins putting together his Indian suit to come out with Fi Yi Yi for his 50th year of masking. *Opposite page:* The back of a beaded patch from the 50th anniversary suit.

Victor: My son, Lil Vic, wanted to make a suit for my 50th year. This photograph looks peaceful, but, man, he came at the last minute with half of nothing. Late and too far behind.

Victor, Jr.: I had only two months to put the suit together. I know I put them under the gun. It hurts I can't mask like I want to—I'm talking about deep down inside—but I've got to provide for my family. Monday through Saturday, I go to work at five o'clock in the morning at an oil refinery. Leading up to Carnival, I was driving to New Orleans every weekend after work to sew.

Victor: Wow, it was rough. We had to stay in day-in and day-out to finish. He brought so much stress on Jack and me! Jack said, "I'm only one person!!"

Victor, Jr.: My style is like the regular downtown Indians.

Jack: Lil Vic wanted a crown like a lot of the younger guys in the neighborhood, but I don't know how to make a crown. I make masks. I kept working on Vic's suit and Vic worked on Lil Vic's. I told him, "You're a good Indian and everything, but you need to start earlier!"

Victor: Jack won't stay overnight unless we are at the very end. I'll fuss at him: "I don't want to hear that, bra. You know if Coach were here, he wouldn't be going."

"That's Coach!"

Coach and I would be up overnight. When I got stressed, he'd say, "Rest your mind." We took turns falling asleep under the table.

Jack: I'm still sewing but I tell everyone, "When I retire, I will fully retire. I will go to Texas to be with my grand-children." I love my tribe, though. They give me headaches, but I love them.

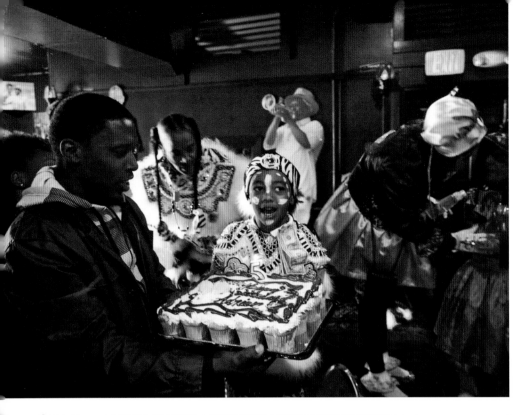

Top: Dijonaise Harris's oldest son, Adrian, celebrates his birthday at the Mother-in-Law with his stepfather, Kenneth Humble, and Big Queen Cutie, Kim Boutte, before he comes out with the tribe on Carnival day.
Bottom: Spyboy Al Polit created a suit in honor of his wife who passed away from breast cancer after struggling with her insurance coverage. He meets Diane Honore Destrehan, founder of the Black Storyville Baby Dolls, in front of the Mother-in-Law Lounge.

Dijonaise: I was 16 when I got pregnant with Adrian. He wasn't even two months old when my dad brought him out to the New Orleans Jazz and Heritage Festival and held him up above the crowd. He's been with Fi Yi Yi ever since. This Carnival, it was his birthday.

Christine: It was good to see Adrian so excited; he loves to be with Victor.

Dijonaise: I stopped masking, but I want all three of my kids to experience it like I did.

Christine: We ask Dijonaise all the time about masking again. The baby dolls have been asking her to come with them, too, which would continue a legacy in our family that started with my grandmother, Big Queen Anita. All I tell her is, "Know the meaning of what you're doing."

Jack Robertson and Wesley Phillips come out of Kermit Ruffins's Mother-in-Law Lounge on Carnival day.

Jack: For the 50th anniversary, I was glad we were out early. That is our hardest problem. I always hope we can get out before noon, but most of the time we are later than that. Chief ain't leaving until everyone's ready to go, and we have a lot of children we have to dress.

My mom and sister say, "You do all that sewing and you don't want to mask?" I tell them, "I'm going to be famous with my artwork." I put my heart and soul into making the suit look different every year. Other Indians say, "Y'all sew too hard," but we're trying to bring the standards up.

155

Victor Harris as the Spirit of Fi Yi Yi comes out on Carnival day with his son, Victor Harris, Jr.

Victor, Jr.: All and all, I made it. My style is different than my daddy's, but I still used cowrie shells to coordinate with Fi Yi Yi. The shells are in my elephant head and throughout a lot of my designs. I wanted to let my father know, "I'm here. I'm not out of town working on Mardi Gras." All these Indians have their sons, and they love to showboat their children. The other Indians look for me, and I know it's a hell of a feeling for my daddy to have us be together.

Left: Wildman Ronald Dumas wearing his buffalo mask at Kermit Ruffins's Mother-in-Law Lounge on Carnival day. *Right:* Ronald Dumas and Renée Rome before leaving the Mother-in-Law Lounge.

Ronald: I put a mask over my face for Chief's anniversary. It is not for the wild buffalo of the Plains Indians sacred to many Mardi Gras Indians, but for the memory of the buffalo that used to roam in Louisiana. I also wanted to honor the cattle around Vacherie, which means "cowshed" in French.

Where I am from, there is a spot around Bayou Boeuf called Maligé that's very spiritual. A lot of winter birds migrate into that area. The old people could tell the coming weather by what bird would ride on the back of the cattle: a late hurricane, a hard winter, or an early spring.

For the suit, I beaded two five point stars and skull and cross bones. The stars represent all the flags of the nation. The message of the skull and cross bones takes us back into history. The privateers and slave catchers tried to take away our humanity, but through my third eye, I won't allow anyone to reduce me to slavery.

Renée Rome: My connection to Ronald has always been a learning process. My family is from Vacherie, and we got to know each other through studying genealogy together. He was the one who told me a lot about who I was.

Ronald: Renée's last name is Rome. In Vacherie, wherever the Rome was, the Dumas was. Wherever the Dumas was, the Rome was. There was a lot of passing of culture, family, and secrets because of skin color. But there was a time when there was harmony, and people were all right with it. This time produced a lot of us. These cultures came together and created something good. Renée and I look back into that window.

Renée: As a friend, Ronald took me into Fi Yi Yi. When he brought me into Tremé, we went into St. Augustine Catholic Church, and started attending the drum circles. That's where I first saw Chief. He was strong-minded. He scared me, but then I saw the kindness in him. Every year, before Carnival, he asks me, "Renée, do you have a feather?"

Ronald: Renée supports the tribe with pictures, time, and voluntary contributions. I asked Chief if I could bead something for her in honor of his 50 years of masking.

Renée: I was a little leery of a crown on my head. I didn't know if I was worthy. I still don't know what my position is, but the tribe has accepted me. They've placed me somewhere.

Big Chief of the Yellow Pocahontas, Darryl Montana, with his mother, Joyce Montana, greets Fi Yi Yi at the Montana home on North Villere in the Seventh Ward. Darryl is wearing a "triple crown," which had never been put on the street before. He said it was so heavy it was difficult to wear.

Darryl Montana: Not having a position doesn't mean you don't have a place. I masked 15 years under my daddy until I got a position. I couldn't meet nobody because I didn't have a title, but I was committed to him and the tribe. I wanted to be part of it.

There are cycles that continue, and others that we move on from. My daddy told me there were things his father was right about, but he didn't get a chance to tell him. There were things my daddy told me that I didn't get a chance to thank him for either. But I do feel good that my mom has

been here to witness all my years of masking. There is no way I would be able to do it without her. Whenever I felt like I was going to quit, I would say to myself, "As long as my mama is here, I'll keep going."

A few years after this picture was taken, in 2017, I told her, "Joyce, you know, this is going to be my last time." She said, "Well, if that's what you feel." I've been doing this since I was nine years old, and there are other things I want to do.

Shaka Zulu: Masking with Darryl, I have been an understudy of one of the greatest chiefs of all time. I have gotten to know the man, the teacher, and the spirit of the Pocahontas tribe.

Darryl: When I showed Shaka how to sew many years ago, I spilled my guts because I wanted to be cut loose. I wanted to be able to keep creating and not get pulled into helping him with his suit every year.

Shaka: I am really proud to be one of the people chosen to carry on such a powerful legacy. I knew Tootie, but I never had a chance to sit down with him. But Darryl taught me much of Tootie's history and how it influenced his life.

Darryl: What I've learned is that to be a chief, you have to know how to lead, you've got to carry yourself in a respectable manner locally and abroad, and you've got to know how to do your craft: draw, sew, sing, and dance. Shaka fires on all cylinders. He has been with me the longest. I believe fair is fair.

Shaka: I have joined a long lineage, and I know there will be more after me. Darryl gave me the opportunity to look at leadership through my own lens.

Darryl: In my lifetime of being involved in the culture, I never witnessed a chief passing a tribe onto someone else until it happened to me. When my daddy passed on the Yellow Pocahontas on North Villere, we went to Congo Square and had a ceremony. I felt I had to go to the beginning. I don't think it's written where you should receive it, but I told Shaka to bring the drums to my parents' home on North Villere. From there, he can take the tribe anywhere.

Shaka Zulu masking on Carnival day with the Yellow Pocahontas. In 2018, Darryl Montana plans to pass on the tribe to Shaka.

The Spirit of Fi Yi Yi and the Mandingo Warriors
meet Jerome Smith, co-founder Tambourine & Fan,
at the Mardi Gras Indian Council's Super Sunday
parade. *Front to back:* Victor Harris, Kim Boutte,
Rob Salter, and Jack Robertson.

Jack: Some people have told me, "Mr. Jack, I didn't talk
to you because you look so mean. You got to smile more!"
But people speak to me on the street a lot more than they
used to. I guess they are starting to realize I'm not no hard
person to get a long with. Even people like Jerome Smith
know what my role in the tribe is.

Now that everyone knows I sew, they want to ask for advice
or want me to sew for them. I say, "You can't sew like Fi Yi
Yi, you have to sew like you sew."

Victor Harris, Jr. dressed in the Elephant suit for Super Sunday.

Victor: I asked Lil Vic how he was going to take over the tribe when he worked so much. He said, "I'm going to take over when you stop masking." I said, "I'll let you know when I stop masking. If you going to wait for that, you going to be waiting for a minute."

Victor, Jr.: I will be the big chief after my father. Even if I have to get another job, I will sacrifice so that the legend can live on. The first year, I will have to mask in black to honor my dad's start in 1984. But for his 50th year, I chose a hot color. I had so many pink feathers left over, a light came on after Super Sunday. My daddy said, "Well, son, I'm going to use the rest of these. Next year, I'll mask in pink."

2 0 1 6

Christine and Victor Harris with their daughter, Dijonaise's son, Kenneth Humble, Jr.

Janet Sula Evans, Medicine Queen of the Mandingo Warriors: In the African tradition I was initiated in, you are often called to accept your own priesthood through illness. I myself did not accept this call until I was diagnosed with breast cancer in 2007. You can also be called unto people through illness. I wanted to join the Spirit of Fi Yi Yi because he represented Africa. But then people in the community told me Victor was sick with shingles. I prayed for him. I left messages on his voicemail asking how he was doing, and mentioned I was interested in joining his tribe. He would never call me back. I still prayed for him.

One day, after about a year of trying, I was doing spiritual work in my shrine. The sky was a deep blue with intense white clouds. I was told in spirit, "Put on your whites and go see him." It felt very deliberate. I went over to Chief's house with my book, *Spirits of the Orisha*, and knocked on the door. He said, "Who is this?"

"It's Sula. I came to bring you a copy of my book. And while I'm here, I need to know, today, if I can be in your tribe. I'm a queen without a king. I need to know if you can cover me or not."

He looked at me in shock. Without saying yes or no, he put supplies in front of me: "Here are some beads. The color this year is pink."

But this was just the first step. I knew I had to meet the whole tribe and the royal Fi Yi Yi family—the clan, the village. I wanted to respectfully come in. That first year, Dijonaise was pregnant with her second son, Kenneth. I am a birth doula. I connected with the whole family over anticipating his birth.

Christine: Ms. Sula can say some real sweet things to you and make you feel good.

Left: Medicine Queen Sula Evans walks through Tremé on Carnival day with Rob Salter and Ricky Gettridge accompanying her on bass drum and tambourine. *Right:* Sula Evans's beaded apron dedicated to Oshun, orisha of love and the river in the Yoruba religion.

Cinnamon Black: Kim, how do you feel to have more queens?

Kim: I like it. I had my little queens, and I guess it was time to get some adults.

Sula: I always loved Big Queen Kim from Queens of the Nation, and I've known Cinnamon for almost 20 years.

Kim: I like Sula, too. She is joyful.

Jack: Sula tries to keep us in check.

Kim: She can be shy, but she does a little dancing. She dances more like a warrior.

Sula: I had to call on the spirit of my grandmothers and face myself. I realized I didn't have to be tough to hold my place. I could just be Sula, Woman of Peace. Once we got to know each other, I really loved standing next to those queens. It was like being initiated into a girl gang. I've got their back and they've got mine. We all have our individual commitments to bringing the spirit.

Cinnamon Black: I like how Sula comes out with her smoke.

Sula: I use frankincense, which is a purification incense.

Christine: Have you seen how Sula sews? She is really talented.

Left: Voodoo Baby Doll Second Queen Resa "Cinnamon Black" Bazile. ***Right:*** Sula Evans without her mask.

Sula: I am a painter, but a Mardi Gras Indian queen named Elenora Rukiya Brown showed me how to sew beaded patches.

Jack: Sula can sew, now. She takes it to another level.

Cinnamon Black: Her suits are specifically about the spiritual.

Sula: My suits are based on African goddess figures and symbols of power from Africa. For the pink suit, I sewed Oshun, the orisha of love and the river.

Cinnamon Black: I was ordained here, but Sula was ordained in Ghana, West Africa. She and I are both vodou priestesses. God speaks different languages. When the spirit speaks through Fi Yi Yi, everyone will hear it.

Kim: Victor comes as a warrior.

Cinnamon Black: Just listen to the drums.

Sula: When I walk next to Chief, it feels like we are walking with thunder under our feet.

167

Big Chief Victor Harris approaches the Backstreet Cultural Museum as the Spirit of Fi Yi Yi on Carnival day.

Spyboy Al Polit rides Geronimo under the I-10 overpass on North Claiborne Avenue with Wildman Ronald Dumas in front of him. In 2016, Ronald sewed a beaded apron.

Ronald: Our spyboy, Polit, has a high, high spirit.

Al: I never thought about being afraid. You got to meet everything head on.

Ronald: In the church, if you see someone slain in the spirit, you get scared because you think they might tear things up. This can be how Polit is on the street.

Al: Leading up to Carnival, I got into an accident and couldn't wear my full crown. I had to tone it down a little bit. I put on my buckskin suit with a war bonnet. I said, "If I can't walk, I'm going to get a horse." My cousin Cooper runs the stable for Charbonnet Funeral Home under the highway along St. Peter Street, and his horse, Geronimo,

lives there, too. Geronimo is a parade horse. He bows to get me and can dance to anything, including motorcycle tribes. He mixed right into our tribe because he pulls the horse-drawn buggies for the jazz funerals.

On Geronimo, I was really able to go scouting for Chief. I had a better view of who was coming, and how big of a tribe they had. When I returned, I got off the horse to meet Chief eye-to-eye. If he threw the signal to gather up, we knew we were getting ready to meet another tribe.

Throughout the day, a lot of Indians told me they had thought about doing something similar. One spyboy from the Ninth Ward said, "Man, that's nice. I was going to do that! Keep the drive alive." He made me blush all over the place.

2017

Victor Harris as the Spirit of Fi Yi Yi comes out of Joan Rhodes's home in Tremé on Carnival day. Joan Rhodes was the catalyst behind Sylvester Francis starting the Backstreet Cultural Museum in the old Blandin Funeral Home.

Spyboy Ricky Gettridge: I've known Victor since we were young. We both come from the Yellow Pocahontas. I was Tootie's spyboy for nine years. I also worked on jobs with Chief where he was the lather and I was the plasterer. We swung stages together on many construction sites. I stopped masking in 1969, but kept parading with different organizations. It was Uncle Lionel Batiste who suggested that I hook up with Cinnamon Black and become a baby doll.

Cinnamon Black: Uncle Lionel's family started the Tremé Million Dollar Baby Dolls. He said I was dressed the same way they used to mask. He decided to pass the name onto me, but still wanted to be involved, and this is how we started the tradition of having men baby dolls. Uncle Lionel held an audition and picked out the girls who were going to dance with me. On Carnival day, we paraded with the Tremé Brass Band. Other men of jazz like Al "Carnival Time" Johnson and Oswald "Bo Monkey" Jones, who is a grand marshal for the Tremé, joined us as well.

Ricky: I watched Cinnamon switching from being the queen of the Tremé Million Dollar Baby Dolls to being a marvelous Indian queen. It was through my closeness with her that I began following Fi Yi Yi.

Cinnamon Black: Ricky had stopped sewing. I asked him, "Rick, you know how to sew and you know how to sing, why don't you do your own thing this year for Carnival?" I took him to store and helped him order all of his materials.

Ricky: It was no complete suit, but I sewed a crown to go along with the rest of the baby dolls.

Kim: Ricky is not a member of Fi Yi Yi, but he's like family.

Cinnamon Black: First you have to become family before you become a member. He sewed in support of the baby dolls, but also the chief. And Ricky can sing.

Kim: He knows all the old songs.

Ricky: I learned them when my daddy used to hold Indian practice in our yard for the Eighth Ward Hunters. I'm glad to still be around to share those songs. When I'm holding two tambourines, it reminds me of a song they used to sing about me:

The police stood on Canal Street
blowing his police whistle.
And here is comes Spyboy Ricky
from the Yellow Pocahunter gang,
and hit him with two shiny pistols,
Talking about, "Hey hey,"
Jock-a-mo fino, "Hey hey."

Victor loves to have the message through the drums. Occasionally he'll tell you, "Nothing but drums," and he won't want to hear no singing. But then he'll call on me, "Okay Spy, sing your number."

Victor Harris and Fred Johnson on Carnival under the bridge on North Claiborne Avenue.

Victor: When I hear the old songs Spyboy Ricky sings, it reminds me of my time with the Yellow Pocahontas. It's still in my blood. As I was completing this book, I felt like I needed to talk to Fred Johnson, who I grew up with in the Yellow Pocahontas, about what had happened between us when I was forced to split more than 30 years ago.

Fred: When it happened, we were young. George Bernard Shaw: "Youth is wasted on the young." We don't know. We think we know, but as we try to create our own reputations, we are often influenced by other people. We misunderstand the full meaning of principles and friendship.

Victor: Over the years, we've come back together for so many events in the community, but we never talked about what happened.

Fred: Victor, as I matured as a man, nobody has been able to tell me anything negative about you. As a young man, they might have been able to tell me something. But I say to your face and behind your back, when you look at it from a historical perspective, there hasn't been anybody after Tootie who masked consistently as many years but you. The other dudes we were masking with didn't develop a consistent record, year in, year out. The truth of the matter is, back then, some of the main naysayers who had a problem with you never masked at all.

Victor: I prayed so hard that I needed help from God—no other—and he invested this in me. I still love you and everyone we masked with.

Fred: That Yellow Pocahontas changed, too. Nothing's going to stay the same. How many years have you masked, Victor?

Victor: 52.

Fred: As time goes on, it's a harder and harder commitment to keep. I know it because even though I don't mask anymore, I put Black Men of Labor's second line on the street each year. You and I still have something in common with Sudan Social and Pleasure Club and the other people we were raised up with: We keep going because we really believed in what Tootie Montana taught us.

Victor: This year I'm going beyond, in terms of our chief. He did it for 52 years, and now he is telling me to move on; keep going. Don't stop. Tootie is passing the ball to me. I'm about to set the bar higher. Continuous 53 years in 2018.

Darryl Montana: Vic is a hell of a sewist, but what I respect about him most of all is that he created his own identity. A lot of guys dress in ways, it appears to me, that try to be the person they admire. Vic created his own legacy. He didn't stay in a box. He created his own.

Shaka Zulu: One day I envision Yellow Pocahontas coming together with Fi Yi Yi to honor his beginnings, and to also know that he has a place in the Yellow Pocahontas tribe. Coming from a masking culture myself, I recognize we are not always present in a human form. People really respect the entity Victor has created; it's bigger than him. It's the transformation from human to spirit.

Victor Harris as the Spirit of Fi Yi Yi comes out for Super Sunday with a second mask.

177

HOW WE DID IT

Rachel Breunlin, Bruce Sunpie Barnes, Cynthia Becker,
Jeffrey David Ehrenreich, and Helen A. Regis

Left: The Neighborhood Story Project hosts the Joint Reception of the American Anthropological Association conference in New Orleans in 2010. ***Right:*** With the support of the New Orleans Musicians' Clinic, the Spirit of Fi Yi Yi and the Mandingo Warriors perform at the reception. Photographs by Jeffrey David Ehrenreich.

Intellectual Lineages

Rachel: I produced this collaborative ethnography with my teacher. Jeffrey Ehrenreich saw me through a Master's program in urban studies at the University of New Orleans. He always wanted me to go on to earn a doctoral degree. He said it would provide more security in my future as a scholar, but I believe it was more than that.

Jeffrey: I've thought a lot about our intellectual families, our lineages.

Rachel: Jeffrey cares deeply about the genealogies of intellectual traditions. When I decided to co-found the Neighborhood Story Project rather than continue on with graduate school, he mourned that I would not write a dissertation, the rite of passage required by the discipline to be placed in a direct line back to the beginnings of anthropology. He knew without one there would be no shorthand to explain where I fit in. Still, Jeffrey didn't give up on me, and his ongoing mentorship and support ultimately led to this book. We could have produced it without telling the story behind it, but in the spirit of Collins "Coach" Lewis, I thought it was important to tell how we did it. As we have worked on a book full of

ancestors, I wanted to recognize the ones we share, and how we have tried to honor them and the relationships that go into co-creation (Haviland 2017).

Jeffrey: In my training as an anthropologist, I had many teachers who were significant. I told Rachel that they are her intellectual grandparents and great grandparents. There was the irascible Stanley Diamond (2017 [1974]), but there is also Michael Harner, who grew up in Greenwich Village in New York City and considers himself to be a scientist who personally and academically deals with the realm of the spirit (1980). His laugh is infectious. He is an engaged listener, a spiritual leader. He eventually gave up his academic career to start the Foundation for Shamanic Studies, where I am now a board member, to recover shamanic knowledge around the world.

In our line of work, books shape lives as much as living people. Long dead anthropologists can come back to life as ancestors. I first read the words of anthropologist Dorothy Lee, a Greek immigrant born in Constantinople, in classes I took with her friend and close colleague, Edmund Carpenter. I never met her; she died in 1976. But her book

Freedom and Culture (1987 [1959]) had a huge impact on the way I have taught and the ethics of my own life. When I realized that both it and another one of her books, *Valuing the Self* (1986 [1976]), were out of print, I worked to have them republished. These books are both about trying to hold on to the best of ourselves, to remember what the human condition is really about.

Rachel: When I wrote my Master's thesis on a small jazz club in Tremé called Joe's Cozy Corner (2004), Jeffrey told me to read *Valuing the Self*, which documents the importance of learning from cultures that provide social spaces and experiences for individuals to value themselves and others. Throughout graduate school, I was lucky to be part of many organizations that cultivated these experiences, which ultimately helped me produce this ethnography. While teaching writing in Jim Randels's and Kalamu ya Salaam's Students at the Center program at John McDonogh Senior High, I was inspired to join an organization called Education Not Incarceration. At the time, the United States's prison population had grown from 230,000 incarcerated people in 1970 to over two million in 2000. For some broader context, in 2000, Canada had a prison population of 31,000 and Mexico a population of 160,000. If Louisiana were a country, it would have the highest rate of incarceration in the entire world. The reality of these statistics was glaring at John Mac; everyone knew someone who was in prison. Many young people had already been themselves.

In 2003, one of my best friends from graduate school, Melissa Burch, recruited members of Education Not Incarceration to help her organize Critical Resistance South, a conference working to end the prison industrial complex. On the opening night at the Tremé Community Center, Reverend David "Goat" Carson gave an invocation. He began by asking us to laugh, but we didn't feel like doing it. Everyone had just gotten there, many of us didn't know each other, and that's not what we wanted to do. We looked around sheepishly trying to figure out how to begin, if at all, and the first sounds out of people were stilted. But that in itself was funny, and something began to build. The laughter became real. The gymnasium erupted. It was an uprising of laughter.

The same evening, Ashley Hunt presented a short film, "Organizing Critical Resistance South," that included a flash of images of social justice organizing in the South from Ida B. Well's anti-lynching campaigns, to the multiracial Southern Tenant Farmers Union, to the Civil Rights and Black Power Movements, and the fight against the prison-industrial complex. Sitting in the gymnasium, I felt proud to be part of this lineage. Jerome Smith, the

Cultural anthropologists Rachel Breunlin and Helen Regis wait for the Spirit of Fi Yi Yi and the Mandingo Warriors on St. Joseph's night at Kermit Ruffins's Mother-in-Law Lounge in 2016. Photograph by Jeffrey David Ehrenreich.

co-founder and director of Tambourine & Fan, was another speaker. In explaining what it was like to grow up in the neighborhood, he said: "When I was a little boy we jumped out of the first floor window of Craig Elementary to follow the band!" His experience claimed a different intellectual history that diverged from the classroom and moved into the streets. I was interested because Joe's Cozy Corner was a frequent second line stop, and my role in the conference was to organize a parade with the Tremé Sidewalk Steppers Social and Pleasure Club and the New Birth Brass Band. At the end of the parade, Papa Joe greeted former Black Panther Angela Davis and hundreds of other second liners by offering them bowls of red beans and rice. Later that evening, young children stood in the doorway, dancing on the sidewalk to Kermit Ruffins and the Barbecue Swingers playing in the back room.

It was years of these convergences in activism, music, and teaching that inspired me to imagine working in the city with the rigor of academia and the spirit of transformation I had been experiencing through community organizing. As if to reaffirm the possibility of doing both, it was at the Critical Resistance South's parade that I met Helen Regis, an anthropologist and friend of Jeffrey's who studied second lines (Regis 1999, 2001). Helen joined my thesis committee and, a few years later, became a board member of the NSP where she serves as our series editor. What this means is really precious to me and the organization. From our first conversations in front of the barroom, Helen and I have shared writing and research together in a way that often reminds me of how Jack and Victor share the creation of designs on a Fi Yi Yi suit. Over and over again, I've put her ethnography and critical histories of parades, photography, and life histories to work in the way we have constructed our books at the NSP.

Life Histories

Helen: I got to know Jeffrey when we organized a session on life histories at the American Anthropological Association's conference in New Orleans. Our panel included presentations on cultural activists Reverend Goat, Marie Laveau, Allison Miner, Sally Ann Glassman, and others. Many of the New Orleanians who had contributed interviews were in the audience and participated in a dialogue that explored the intersection of humanistic and social science approaches to ethnography, the importance of narrative, and how we've all struggled with the oppressive social structures in which we are often enmeshed. The dialogues that began at the conference convinced me to develop a life history course at Louisiana State University.

Rachel: Jeffrey was beginning to teach a life history course at UNO as well. Although I was finished with coursework, I bought all the required books and read them anyway. The first was Paul Radin's *Autobiography of a Winnebago Indian* (1963).

Jeffrey: I discovered Paul Radin, an outsider in the world of academia, through Stanley Diamond. He came from a family of scholars and rabbis from Germanic Poland and got his degree from Columbia University in 1911. He believed that you could understand a culture through life history and did 17 years of fieldwork with the Winnebago Indians between the academic jobs that he never held for long. He wrote a series of autobiographies and ethnographic accounts with the Winnebago. Stanley Diamond admired his humanistic point of view so much he wrote introductions to Radin's books, and edited *Culture in History: Essays in Honor of Paul Radin* (1960).

Rachel: Radin believed in the particulars of people's lives; the poetic complications that existed there. Reading his work, I became interested in learning how to use ethnography to become a medium—to be able to listen deeply, record, and translate experience for broader audiences. I read other books Jeffrey had assigned as well: *Mama Lola* (McCarthy Brown 1992), *Writing Women's Worlds* (Abu-Lughod 1993), and *Translated Woman* (Behar 1993). When I graduated and began editing the first round of Neighborhood Story Project books, I drew upon their methods of editing to figure out how to create multi-vocal, collaborative ethnographies.

Helen: One of the main books I remember Jeffrey recommending was Barbara Myerhoff's *Number Our Days* (1978). He presented her work as this important intervention that anticipated the postmodern critique of anthropology that directly addressed questions of power

in authorship. Barbara was one of the early ethnographers to write about a community that was associated with whiteness in the United States. In her portrait of an elderly Jewish community in Venice, California struggling against gentrification, she unpacks an incredibly rich cultural history and quotes people she works with asking her hard questions about the goals of ethnography and her own Jewish identity.

Rachel: My favorite part of the book was Barbara's friendship with Shmuel. He was an internationalist, a socialist, and philosopher. Over the years, I've taught a passage from him in my classes:

> Now I will tell you about culture. Culture is that garden. This is not a thing of nations. It is not about Goethe and yeshivas. It is children playing. Culture is the simple grass through which the wind blows sweetly and each grass blade bends softly to the caress of the wind. It is like a mother who would pick up her child and kiss it, with her tenderness that she gave birth to it. We don't see this anymore. In the present time, we see nations. They are not natural outgrowings. Their roots are too harsh. They grew up too fast. They have not got that natural sweetness. [Myerhoff 1978:60]

In some ways, Shmuel's vision is utopian but in others it fits into Dorothy Lee's and Jeffrey's interests in how we can create lives that are satisfying to human beings; what conditions bring out the best in us. I wanted to create texts that could be part of the garden, not just the yeshiva. At the time, I was running an independent media project called New Orleans Public Forum, teaching at John Mac and working at the Women's Center at the University of New Orleans. Trying to figure out my route forward, I read everything from Paulo Freire's books on popular education (2000) to Ishmael Reed's "Neo-HooDoo Manifesto," which proclaimed: "Neo-HooDoo believes that every man is an artist and every/artist's a priest. You can bring your own creative ideas to Neo-HooDoo" (Reed 1972).

And then I encountered Deborah A. Gordon's essays in *Women Writing Culture*, which situated social justice activism, feminist ethnography, and the constraints of academia in ways that deeply resonated with me. She called out alternative publishing efforts like Aunt Lute Press, which publishes and distributes books "that have the educational potential to change and expand social realities" (Gordon 1995: 438). I decided developing infrastructure to redistribute educational privilege and create ethnographies that live in the communities being represented was more of my calling than getting another degree. When fellow teacher in the Students at the Center program and DIY publisher, Abram Himelstein, said he was starting the Neighborhood Story Project with the mission of "Our stories told by us," I said I would join him.

In 2004, Jeffrey hired me to teach a class for the UNO Department of Anthropology while Abram and I got the NSP off the ground. When I asked the College of Liberal Arts if they would support a position for me to co-direct the organization, Jeffrey, as chair, said that it could be housed in Anthropology. With the department's support of collaborative ethnography and community-based publishing, Abram and I set up a workshop on Lapeyrouse Street in the Seventh Ward, a few blocks away from John Mac and my house.

African Art History in New Orleans

Helen: After Hurricane Katrina, Jeffrey really dived into photographing Fi Yi Yi. It was a time when there were layers upon layers of documentation happening around the tribe. Lisa Katzman was working on *Tootie's Last Suit* (2005), Claire Tancons was curating an exhibit at the New Orleans Museum of Art for Prospect.1, and Aaron Walker was filming *Bury the Hatchet* (2010). Lisa and Jeffrey worked closely together and discussed the importance of life narratives in how we understand Mardi Gras Indians in the city. In her film, she showed vulnerabilities that hadn't been put into the public realm before. In discussing how their personal experiences intersect the tradition of masking, the Montana family revealed some of the most tender experiences in their lives.

Not everyone was comfortable with that. When the film came out, some people in the Mardi Gras Indian community argued that those stories should be kept private. But the film was part of opening up a conversation about how suits are made with communities: the friendships and family relationships that go into making those suits, and the many hours around the kitchen table. One of the most powerful moments was watching Tootie go to work, walking down the sidewalk by himself with his tool bag.

Rachel: There is another scene I love where the wildman of the Mandingo Warriors, Kenneth Lewis, is following Tootie and Joyce Montana as they leave the Circle Food Store. I am endeared to the intersection of a banal trip to make groceries with the ceremonial dancing and chanting of the Yellow Pocahontas and Fi Yi Yi. Working and living in New Orleans, these juxtapositions happen a lot.

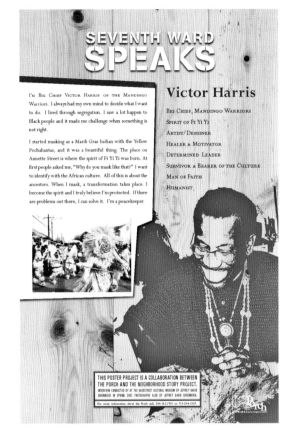

The Neighborhood Story Project and the Porch 7th Ward Cultural Organization partnered to create a series of portraits of residents of the Seventh Ward, which included Victor Harris. Poster courtesy of the Neighborhood Story Project with photographs by Jeffrey David Ehrenreich.

Helen: At the time, Rachel and I were also part of a collective of residents and artists called the Porch 7th Ward Cultural Organization. It was through the Porch that we created a poster series called "Seventh Ward Speaks" based on collaborative interviews that highlighted creativity and activism in our neighborhood (Breunlin and Regis 2009).

Rachel: As part of the project, we worked with Jeffrey to put together a poster honoring the Spirit of Fi Yi Yi. I also worked with Willie Birch on an interview with his best friend, visual artist Ron Bechet, at Willie's studio in the Seventh Ward. In their discussion of African American art, Ron told stories of Robert Farris Thompson's lectures at Yale University—learning about the importance of claiming African retentions in contemporary African American art, and being brought into the multi-sensory experiences of African drumming in Thompson's classroom. Right on time, at the opening of "Seventh Ward Speaks," the Spirit of Fi Yi Yi and the Mandingo Warriors showed up with their own drums. Listening to their rhythms, I remembered Ron recounting how he read Sidney Bechet's autobiography, *Treat It Gentle*, and began appreciating his own family's connection to Africa. In the late 1950s, Sidney Bechet had made them explicitly:

I'm an old man now; I can't keep hanging on... And all I've been waiting for is the music. All the beauty that there's ever been, it's moving inside that music...the voice the wind had in Africa, and the cries from Congo Square, and the fine shouting that came from Free Day. The blues, the spirituals, and the remembering, and the waiting, and the suffering...somehow when the music is played right it does an explaining of all of those things. [Bechet 2002: 218]

Helen: In the 1990s, I moved from New Orleans across the Atlantic ocean to a Fulbe town in Cameroon. Living in a Muslim community did little to prepare me to learn about the connections between the city and art-making in Africa. It wasn't until I had to teach a course on African art and culture at Mississippi State University that I immersed myself in the spirit-filled art, dancing and masquerades of the Yoruba, Dogon, Bamana, Mande, and Kongo. To learn more, I audited a class taught by Dr. Sara Hollis at Southern University of New Orleans. When I started to write about second line parades, I was inspired by how African art historians took performance seriously and chronicled how masquerades reference history and politics, as well as enact their own. Along with Robert Farris Thompson, Henry Drewal and Margaret Drewal's work, the scholarship of Mary Jo Arnoldi, Allen and Mary H. Nooter Roberts, and John W. Nunley helped me to understand what people are up to when they are dancing down the streets (Drewal and Mason 1997; Drewal 1992; and Drewal and Drewal 1990; Arnoldi 1996, Nooter Roberts 1996; Nunley 1999, 1998).

Cynthia: I was drawn to African art history because of these connections as well. A native of the city, I came out of Department of Anthropology at the University of New

Orleans. When I graduated, Professor Malcolm Webb encouraged me to complete my PhD at the University of Wisconsin-Madison, which had a great reputation in African studies. Although the transition to living in the Midwest was tough, the classes that I took with Henry Drewal reminded me of home. Henry specialized in Yoruba art in Nigeria, and his classes and writings brought to life the dynamism and creativity that I experienced growing up in New Orleans. In order to study with him, I switched from anthropology to art history. He taught me to be sensitive to the performative aspects of art, and to pay attention to the interplay between the visual, dance, and music in their ceremonial contexts.

Henry's own lineage was connected to his studies with Robert Farris Thompson, who had coined the term "Black Atlantic" in *Flash of the Spirit* to characterize the visual culture shared by people of African descent on both sides of the Atlantic (1984). In his writing, he often returns to Mardi Gras Indians in New Orleans to make the connections. For instance, in a 2005 essay, "When the Saints Go Marching In: Kongo Louisiana, Kongo New Orleans" that was published in the catalogue, *Resonances from the African Past: African Sculpture from the New Orleans Museum of Art*, he asserted that Mardi Gras Indians, like jazz, gumbo, Voodoo and Creole architecture, represent an amalgamation of Kongo, Mande, and Yoruba-Fon cultures from Africa (Thompson 2011). He compared Mardi Gras Indian suits and their use of feathers to Kongo cultures where feathers refer to confidence and strength, and implied that the use of feathers by Mardi Gras Indians was a cultural retention from Africa that worked to heal the trauma of the Middle Passage.

Rachel: He also spent time comparing the aesthetics found in African sculpture to people's gestures in New Orleans.

Cynthia: When I am at home, I often find myself doing the same thing. In 2009, I saw Victor roaming the streets on Carnival day wearing a red suit and holding an oval shield. The shield featured a beaded face whose symmetrical design and radiating projections resembled a Senufo mask from Ivory Coast in West Africa. Performed by male blacksmiths as part of an initiation ceremony, art historian Anita Glaze wrote that this Senufo facemask was part of a larger multisensory ensemble that included colorful scarves and shawls placed on raffia. Dynamic music accompanied its performance, adding to its energy and magnetism. Male masqueraders from different villages competed with each other, and although women did not mask, they frequently broke from the audience circle to dance in front of a champion masker (Glaze 1986: 34). In the Ivory Coast, this contributed a sense of celebration and community that we also see in Mardi Gras Indians processions.

When the Committee of Fi Yi Yi created a spectacular green-feathered suit in 2011, I saw the Senufo mask appear again in Victor's oval-shaped mask. When I looked at the rounded eyes, they resembled the circular patterns carved around the mask's eyes. Both featured long thin noses that led to gaping mouths with sharp teeth. In addition, the form of his massive collar seemed to draw from the mask's ear-like projections. Unlike the Senufo mask, however, the Fi Yi Yi collar was covered with beaded spiders, referencing Ananse, the trickster spider featured in Ghanaian Ashanti stories and carried to the southern United States as Aunt Nancy. In the diaspora, Ananse represents how the weak can use cleverness and wit to overthrow the powerful and to survive in a racist and dangerous society. The Committee of Fi Yi Yi has created suits that expertly merged various African influences to create works of art that are visually stunning and filled with deep symbolic meaning.

Rachel: At the Porch, we were immersed in similar conversations about memory, retention, magic, and coincidence. In practice, we were looking for ways to bridge continents, neighborhoods, and disciplines in academia. It was through Ron Bechet that we started collaborating with Jan Cohen Cruz, author of *Local Acts: Community-Based Performance in the United States* (2005). Her work around performance was largely based on theater, but, of course, community-based performances in New Orleans were also produced by Indian tribes and other grassroots organizations. We brought these concepts together in a small Seventh Ward Festival that Helen and I produced with Ed Buckner, the president of the Big Seven Social and Pleasure Club. I first got to know Wesley Phillips as we negotiated different prices for whether Victor was going to wear the suit when the Spirit of Fi Yi Yi and the Mandingo Warriors performed.

Afterwards, Collins "Coach" Lewis came around the Porch to check out the other programming and to see whether we had a consciousness of how our work was linked the history of Tambourine & Fan. The Porch hired Coach to run Mardi Gras Indian sewing workshops, but we never had the large numbers of kids found on Hunter's Field. We soon learned how fleeting cultural organizations can be if the collective doesn't submit their individual egos. This was something Coach knew. When I met with him at his apartment to begin working on this book, he showed me a large Tupperware container full of beaded patches that he had worked on—the proof of his labor. When I asked him what he was going to do with them, he said they could be an inheritance. The patches have stayed with his family, and his perspective on how art and community building happen became one of the primary frameworks for this book.

Dialoging with *African Arts*

Helen: After Hurricane Katrina, Jeffrey and I both spent time in the city supporting grassroots museums. He was on the board of the Backstreet Cultural Museum and worked closely with the Mardi Gras Indian Hall of Fame. I was on the board of another museum called the House of Dance & Feathers in the Lower Ninth Ward (see Breunlin and Lewis 2009; Regis, Breunlin, and Lewis 2011).

Rachel: In 2007, the Neighborhood Story Project received a Louisiana Endowment for the Humanities grant to produce a catalogue for the House of Dance & Feathers. Through the NSP, I had been learning how to create books that incorporated the aesthetics and ethics of New Orleans participatory cultures, but I hadn't worked with a museum before. I was not a trained curator or art historian. I met with Bill Fagaly, an African art curator at the New Orleans Museum of Art (NOMA), who had put together *He's the Prettiest: A Tribute to Big Chief Tootie Montana's 50 years of Mardi Gras Indian Suiting* (1997), to ask his advice about translating the material culture of Mardi Gras Indians into a book format.

Cynthia: From an art history point of view, *He's the Prettiest* was an important step in recognizing the artwork of Mardi Gras Indians. For a long time, most people viewed them as doing "low art" or "craft" rather than works of art worthy of museum display. In the mid-1980s, Bill shocked participants in an art fair in the suburbs of New Orleans by awarding the prize for "best of show" to Larry Bannock, big chief of the Golden Star Hunters. Even in the city itself, people like watching and photographing the Indians, but they are often not recognized as fine artists.

Rachel: For the catalogue to *He's the Prettiest*, Bill asked Kalamu ya Salaam to write an essay about Tootie Montana. Kalamu began his introduction by directly challenging the distinctions made in the art world with the declaration, "All art is folk art" (ya Salaam 1997).

Helen: As Rachel started doing the literature review for the catalogue, I gave her a copy of Henry Drewal's *Beads, Body, and Soul: Art and Light in the Yoruba Universe* (1997).

Cynthia: When Henry curated the exhibition for *Beads, Bodies, and Soul* at the University of Wisconin's art museum with Baba John Mason, a Lukumi priest and devotee of Obatala from New York City, I had just returned to Madison from two years of fieldwork studying Berber (Amazigh) art in Morocco. Henry's long-term fieldwork experience in Nigeria and John's first-hand experience as a Yoruba religious practitioner brought a unique perspective to the exhibition. It emphasized visualize aesthetic connections between Nigerian-based Yoruba beadwork and Yoruba-inspired art in the Americas. Their collaborative methodology and multisensory approach to art had a major impact on me. The exhibition drew attention to a little-studied aspect of African art—beadwork—and featured a broad diversity of Yoruba arts from Africa and the Americas. It used video and field photographs to contextualize the artwork, including a video of an Egungun masquerade performance.

Like Fi Yi Yi, Egungun masks use cloth and beadwork to honor the ancestors. Their suits concentrate on adornment of the head, which is also a common feature of Yoruba art. For example, the *Beads, Body, and Soul* exhibition showed crowns worn by Yoruba rulers on public occasions. A crown's beaded designs include the faces of ancestors and three-dimensional birds, whose power to fly alluded to the connection with the otherworld. A beaded veil would be attached to a crown on state occasions to cover the ruler's face, signaling his divine nature. The beaded veil de-emphasized his individuality and the ruler became a symbol of divine kingship. There are many similarities between Yoruba crowns that express a connection to the supernatural and the beaded suits worn by the Spirit of Fi Yi Yi.

Rachel: I decided to write to Henry in the hope that he would give us permission to use an example of the beadwork in the House of Dance & Feathers catalogue. He agreed, and said I should meet Cynthia.

Helen: We met Cynthia at Bill Fagaly's home in the French Quarter. Bill is a gracious host. We sat on cushy sofas and he poured drinks. My eyes were drifting to fabrics and shelves full of African artifacts from every nation on the continent—colors and texture in every direction. Bill said he was interested in supporting more documentation on Mardi Gras Indians from an art history point of view.

Rachel: In 2008, the Spirit of Fi Yi Yi and the Mandingo Warriors's exhibit at NOMA for Prospect.1 had continued the project of situating Mardi Gras Indian suits into the art world. Recognizing the importance of the relationship between Fi Yi Yi and the Backstreet, curator Claire Tancons

Unknown Artist, Yoruba, 20th century crown, c. 1920
Glass beads, leather, canvas, wicker
Minneapolis Institute of Art,
The Ethel Morrison Van Derlip Fund 76.29
Photo: Minneapolis Institute of Art

worked with Sylvester Francis to borrow suits from the museum and edited video footage of his films of the tribe. In a review in the *New York Times*, art critic Roberta Smith wrote, "Profuse with hallucinatory patterns and colors and evocations of African masks, [Fi Yi Yi's] suits derail any closed definition of art and artist, as does seeing him in them, in action, in videos and in photographs." In another review in the *New Yorker*, the question of how the suits fit into the concept of art was brought up again:

Their intricate and savage beauty integrates countless insights of aesthetic intelligence, refined over time. "Art" seems too effete a word for such glory. [Schjeldahl 2008: 128]

The reviewers seemed to have no reference point for the world of African art, which habitually defies these Western notions of art-making.

Cynthia: Bill encouraged me to begin a project that incorporated African art history into writing about the art of Mardi Gras Indians. To begin, I asked Rachel and Helen if they'd like to organize a panel for the African Studies Association's conference in New Orleans at the Roosevelt Hotel in 2009. The African Studies Association is considered the leading North American organization devoted to the study of Africa. We felt that local cultural traditions should be represented. Felipe Smith from Tulane University presented on Zulu carnival traditions, Rachel discussed the House of Dance & Feathers, Helen presented on the activists who brought art and music from Benin to the New Orleans Jazz & Heritage Festival, and I discussed the visual history of Mardi Gras Indian suits. Henry served as the discussant, linking the presentations and raising questions. This dialogue served as the basis for our special edition of *African Arts* that we called "Performing Africa in New Orleans" (see Becker, Breunlin and Regis 2013).

Sunpie: Around the same time, Rachel and I were working on our book, *Talk That Music Talk* (Barnes and Breunlin 2014), and I was photographing a lot of second line parades. When she asked me if she could include a few photographs in *African Arts*, I was very excited about the opportunity to have some pictures published in such a prestigious volume.

Rachel: As we began organizing the issue, we didn't realize that the group was going to pull together for a much larger project, but soon afterwards, Jeffrey asked me if I was interested in producing a life history of Fi Yi Yi through the Neighborhood Story Project.

Helen: At this point, Jeffrey has published a number of articles on Fi Yi Yi. In *Shamanic Annual: The Journal of the Foundation for Shamanic Studies*, he presented the work of Fi Yi Yi in a classical anthropological style, where there is a clear distinction between the etic and emic voices, to borrow the words from one of Jeffrey's close colleagues, Marvin Harris. In this style, the ethnographer listens closely to the people they are learning from in the field. In the publications, however, there is great distance in tone because the anthropologist pulls quotations from interviews that are based on conversations, and then writes in a quasi-liturgical style of the academic voice. Anthropologists are accustomed to these different genres, but they are jarring to the uninitiated.

Bruce Sunpie Barnes photographing on Carnival day in front of the Backstreet Cultural Museum with Spyboy Ricky Gettridge looking on. Photograph by Jeffrey David Ehrenreich.

Rachel: I told Jeffrey the NSP book project would have to be different. Everyone's voice would have to be on the same register—his experiences considered ethnographically just like everyone else's. This was a hard thing to say to my teacher, even if it had been years since I had been his student, but Jeffrey doesn't take offense easily. If he thinks it's reasonable, he's willing to try it.

Jeffrey: For me, the format of the Neighborhood Story Project books was an opportunity to bring the voices of the Mandingo Warriors to the forefront of my photography with them. While the work of photography and ethnography is important to me, it was their lives and experiences I was given the privilege of participating in, and they owned it. To do this work on terms that worked for both them and me, it had to be fully collaborative and ethical, in every sense of these words.

Sunpie: I knew Jeffrey in many capacities: as a fellow board member of the Backstreet as well as the photographer/professor and spirit catcher ever present with the Fi Yi Yi who sometimes turned the camera on me when I met the tribe as the cig chief of the Northside Skull and Bone Gang. I remember Coach bragging to me about how they were the only gang with their own personal press corps. I have observed and participated in New Orleans cultural movements for over 30 years and Jeffrey's commitment to document the group's movement and process is unprecedented. He is the only documentarian I know of who has focused on one Carnival group in New Orleans for a decade and a half.

The team the Neighborhood Story Project assembled to create this book included some of my favorite people in the city who have produced important bodies of work around understanding the movement of New Orleans street culture. It was very amazing to witness a gang of streetwise and seasoned anthropologists go after a subject matter near and dear to their hearts. Much like the Indian gangs of the city, this collective group of scholars created a tribe of their own.

Producing *Fire in the Hole*

Rachel: In August of 2011, Jeffrey and I launched the book project with Victor, Jack, Wesley, and Coach. A few weeks later, Coach died unexpectedly. We were all in shock. Jeffrey kept photographing, but it took until November for all of us to come back together to record life histories again. I edited the transcripts, and we read them together to make lists of questions to begin filling in the gaps. My job was to facilitate the storytelling, and I remember Jeffrey getting frustrated with me because I was asking micro-detailed follow-up questions. I had to explain that since the book would be solely in people's own voices, the details were important to create vividness in the text. I also worked with Jack, Wesley, and Victor to create a list of questions to ask Jeffrey. Their interview with him ended up lasting hours because of the easy rapport between everyone. Over all, we produced more than 800 pages of transcripts.

Helen: As we worked on *African Arts*, I thought it would be a good opportunity to share some of this work in progress. For the journal, we included the interview that the Committee of Fi Yi Yi did with Jeffrey as the primary text to accompany his photographs (Breunlin, Ehrenreich, Harris, Lewis, Phillips, and Robertson 2013). This was highly unusual for the journal.

Cynthia: In academic journals like *African Arts*, scholarship typically comes from Western-trained cultural outsiders who engage in on-the-ground research to learn about a specific artistic tradition. Although scholars might spend years in discussion with artists, rarely do we hear the voices of artist-practitioners themselves. The Committee of Fi Yi Yi's conversation with Jeffrey showed how "subjects" understand their relationship with the scholars who photograph and write about them, rather than how "experts" interpret a cultural tradition. Jeffrey's photographs also offered readers a rare look at the process of dressing as an Indian. We included a series of photographs that showed Victor in the process of donning his suit. The layers of fabric, beads, and raffia worn by Victor illustrated just how much effort goes into making it. Most people don't realize the level of commitment required to make a new suit each year.

African art historian Cynthia Becker with Wildman Ronald Dumas of the Mandingo Warriors on Carnival day. Adornment for Carnival connects maskers back to important places in their lives or imagination. Cynthia wears jewelry from Morrocco, where she has done long-term fieldwork, and Ronald is draped in Spanish moss from the wetlands of Louisiana. Photograph by Jeffrey David Ehrenreich.

Rachel: *African Arts* is where the NSP's book project began to come to life. Sometimes you need to have a smaller assignment to help resolve basic creative problems. The first was that searching through images is incredibly time consuming. To prepare for the journal, Cynthia and Helen both met with Jeffrey to look through his photographs. Jeffrey's archive includes over a hundred thousand images of the tribe. It easily gets overwhelming.

In New Orleans, the image of the stoic Mardi Gras Indian in galleries and newspapers has become a cliché in the same way Edward Curtis's American Indian images were mass-produced in previous generations (see, for instance, Faris 2003). As I began to think about what to look for in Jeffrey's images for the book, I was inspired by the writer Sherman Alexie's investigations into how people are aware of these stereotypes and use them for protection and jokes with nods and critiques to the past and future (Alexie 1998). While Jeffrey's archive contains these stoic images, he had quickly gone beyond the stance. In fact, the very nature of Fi Yi Yi has a different energy because of their imagination in Africa.

Cynthia: Victor's suits incorporate materials common to art made in Africa, such as raffia, kente cloth, and cowrie shells. Each one of these acknowledges a connection to African aesthetic values and spiritual beliefs. For example, cowrie shells imported from the Indian Ocean served as a form of currency from the fourteenth to the eighteenth centuries in West and Central Africa. Cowries were so valued that African artists used them to adorn ceremonial masks and royal regalia. Cowries also had mystical significance and Yoruba priests threw them during Ifa divination in order to communicate with the realm of the spirits.

People throughout Africa use fibers from raffia palms to adorn masquerade ensembles and, until the early twentieth century, textiles woven from raffia were so valued that nobility in Central Africa used them as burial shrouds. The kente cloth used in the Fi Yi Yi suits also has deep meaning, as kente was originally woven by the Asante Kingdom to serve as prestige cloth. The patterns were named after proverbs, historical events, and respected chiefs and kings. Until recently, certain patterns were reserved for nobility but today I see people wearing kente as a symbol of ethnic pride.

Rachel: We asked curator Claire Tancons to look through Jeffrey's archive and identify images that would be compelling. I went through her selections to train my eyes to think about different ways of seeing the images. Claire was attracted to the artwork: the beaded patches, the close-ups of hands sewing, and the materials on the table. She pointed out the use of light in Jeffrey's images, dramatic encounters with other Mardi Gras Indians, and intimate moments with other members of the tribe and Victor's family. Although he will occasionally zoom out into the larger context of what's going on around the tribe, Jeffery mostly pays attention to the group and who they encounter. After immersing myself in images of the tribe dressed in different colors each year, I decided it would be good to help the reader dive into the experience of being drenched in these vibrant blues, golds, greens, and hot pinks—how the light on the suits shifts each year depending on the designs, weather, and experiences of the tribe.

With a preliminary plan in place, I worked on weaving the text of the interviews together to create the beginning chapters. As a collective, we went over the text together, and did follow-up interviews until we had developed the important experiences that solidified the tribe, and Jeffrey's role as their photographer. This text became the compass I used to approach the photographs again. As I went through the entire archive, my decision to keep an image was based on two factors: They helped tell the unfolding story of the tribe or were an incredibly beautiful. Perhaps a thousand images made this cut. In this vast archive, there are tens of thousands of other images of the tribe's performances at the New Orleans Jazz and Heritage Festival and live music venues. We decided, however, to primarily concentrate on the creation of the suits, significant life and death events for the tribe, and street performances.

Of course, in the six years we worked on the book, new suits were getting created all the time. The sewing wasn't going to stop so we needed to figure out how to end the book. Initially, I decided to concentrate on ten years of photography from the year after Hurricane Katrina in 2006 to Victor's 50th year of masking. We told the stories of the years before Jeffrey started photographing through Michael P. Smith's archive at The Historic New Orleans Collection and the archives and exhibits at the Backstreet Cultural Museum.

Grassroots Institutions

Cynthia: Museum displays are essential to the appreciation and survival of Mardi Gras Indian artistry for future generations. They can also impact how the public perceives them, since museums validate the artistic significance of a tradition. But museums also need local involvement so that they can speak to the spirituality embedded in wearing a mask and summoning its otherworldly essence, especially for a group such as Fi Yi Yi.

Sunpie: Sylvester created a space at the Backstreet for Fi Yi Yi and the Mandingo Warriors to live beyond the three or four events that normally take place in a year for Mardi Gras Indians. In essence, he created the University of Fi Yi Yi.

Rachel: I asked Sunpie to work with me on the museum section of the book because he has spent so much time there as the president of the board, as well as masking with the Northside Skull and Bone Gang.

Sunpie: Photographing the Backstreet is a bit like photographing one's own living room. I have spent countless days, and some nights, at the museum. I know the length and distance of the rooms and hallways (from walking, for instance, to the bathroom at night with the lights out). I know the objects well, and have seen many of them worn on the streets. But when I spent time photographing the collection, I began to realize that the countless hours of imagination and creativity that went into the designs hold their place even when no one is wearing the suits. When you look at them, they still have the vibrant liveliness of those who took the time to sew and hook them up.

Rachel and I also recorded interviews with Sylvester. I'm used to talking to him casually, but interviewing him was a wild ride. His knowledge around New Orleans street culture is a library unto itself. If you listen closely to the memories he shares, he paints a picture not unlike Shakespeare or Confucius—full of humor, trickery, and sometimes tragedy around prices paid for the sake of having fun for just one day.

Victor Harris's 50th anniversary of masking celebration at Dillard University was organized by Professor Freddye Hill. Members of the Mandingo Warriors behind Victor, from left to right: Janet Sula Evans, Resa "Cinnamon Black" Bazile, Kim Boutte, and Perry Emery. Photograph by Jeffrey David Ehrenreich.

Rachel: Throughout 2016 and 2017, Victor, Jack, Wesley, Sylvester and I gathered numerous times to look through the images I had been collecting for the book. I watched how they responded to the different scenes of themselves: which ones made them laugh or comment, which ones they glazed over. I was also waiting for everyone to have some poignant reflections about Victor's 50th year, so that we could find a good ending to the book. No one said very much. There had been a ceremony at Dillard University organized by Freddye Hill that everyone enjoyed, but the next year loomed ahead. Already, Victor was thinking of other legacies related to his relationship to the Yellow Pocahontas. I didn't realize how significant this was to him until we got close to the 52nd year, the same number of years that Tootie Montana had masked. Victor really wanted to include images from this year. We expanded the book to incorporate them.

With a full draft of images, I followed a similar methodology to the one I developed while working with photographs for the House of Dance & Feathers catalogue (Breunlin 2013) and began to meet with the Mandingo Warriors, Victor's family and neighbors, and members of other tribes to talk about what was going on in the pictures we had selected. It was here that the spirit work of Fi Yi Yi really came together. It was powerful to include the stories of people who had devoted themselves to the same art, who had made major life changes to mask with Fi Yi Yi, and who shared their own journeys that led to meeting the tribe and the museum. It was also chaotic. Rather than recording these conversations, I typed as we talked about the photographs, and we co-created the text that accompanied the images.

I gave this full draft to Jeffrey and Helen, who edited with both the knowledge of the culture being represented and the standards of academia in mind.

Helen: I think one of the hardest things is trying to think about how the stories will read to someone who doesn't know New Orleans. There's so much insider talk. We have our own language for masking, parading, sewing, and the layers upon layers of relationships can be hard to untangle.

Sunpie: Everyone on the editorial committee was concerned about how to create equal balance between the photographs and the text. It is often true that people will visually read a book by concentrating on the images first and then diving into the content of the stories. As photo editor, my goal was to create continuity between the images, old and new, just as the narratives were being tied together in cohesive arcs. To prepare to edit the images, I made an effort to learn about the latest image editing tools used in modern, digital color photography. Working on *Fire in the Hole* gave me a brand new insight into the brilliant world of how you look at color images; they do something different in your sensory system than black and white photography. I tried to balance the light and detail in the photograph with the mood and direction of the storyline.

Rachel: Towards the end of making the book, Victor said that he would like to include the museum his son, Curtis, has been creating for Fi Yi Yi and the Mandingo Warriors in the Ninth Ward. It wasn't completed yet, but during his free-time Curtis had converted a single-family home into a museum that was housing years of work, not just from Victor, but from other members of the tribe. I thought about all of the stories we have included of tribes begetting tribes, anthropologists begetting other anthropologists. In the same way, Sylvester's museum has begotten other museums and influenced countless other creative productions. As people devote their lives to yearly cycles of sewing, they have to find places to store all of it. I imagine, in the future, we will see more museums appearing like neighborhood shrines where people can come in and feel the creative energy that comes together each year to make Carnival and the second line season happen. In the Ninth Ward, where Victor now lives, the spirit work of Fi Yi Yi will find another home. In this epilogue, we have tried to do something similar for the dreams of the ethnographers, poets, maskers, writers, art historians, curators, and filmmakers whose bodies of work were inspiration for the creation of *Fire in the Hole*.

Left: The Spirit of Fi Yi Yi and the Mandingo Warriors museum in the Ninth Ward of New Orleans. *Right:* Victor Harris next to an exhibit that his son, Curtis, installed at the museum. Photographs by Bruce Sunpie Barnes.

Works Cited

Abu Lughod, Lila. 1993. *Writing Women's Worlds: Bedouin Stories.* Berkley: University of California Press.

Alexie, Sherman. 1998. *The Lone Ranger and Tonto First Fight in Heaven.* San Diego: Perennial Press.

Arnoli, Mary Jo and Christine Mullen Kreamer. 1995. *Crowning Achievments: African Arts of Dressing the Head.* Los Angeles: UCLA Fowler Museum of Cultural History.

Barnes, Bruce and Rachel Breunlin. 2014. *Talk That Music Talk: Passing On Brass Band Music the Traditional Way.* New Orleans: Neighborhood Story Project at the University of New Orleans Press.

Bechet, Sidney. *Treat It Gentle.* 2009 (orig. 1960). Cambridge, MA: DaCapo Press.

Becker, Cynthia, Rachel Breunlin, and Helen A. Regis. 2013. "Performing Africa in New Orleans." *African Arts* 46 (2): 12–21.

Behar, Ruth. 1993. *Translated Woman: Crossing the Border with Esperanza's Story.* Boston: Beacon Press.

Breunlin, Rachel. 2013. "Bridge Work: Repatriating Mardi Gras Indian Photography with the House of Dance and Feathers." *African Arts* 46 (2): 50–61.

Breunlin, Rachel, Jeffrey David Ehrenreich, Victor Harris, Collins "Coach" Lewis, Wesley Phillips, and Jack Robertson. 2013. "How We Do It: A Collaborative Interview and Essay." *African Arts* 46 (2): 62–69.

Breunlin, Rachel and Ronald W. Lewis. 2009. *The House of Dance & Feathers: A Museum by Ronald W. Lewis.* New Orleans: Neighborhood Story Project at the University of New Orleans Press.

Breunlin, Rachel and Helen A. Regis. 2009. "Can There Be a Critical Collaborative Ethnography? Creativity and Activism in the Seventh Ward, New Orleans." *Collaborative Anthropologies,* edited by Luke Eric Lassister. 2: 115–146.

Breunlin, Rachel. 2004. *Papa Joe Glasper and Joe's Cozy Corner: Downtown Development, Displacement, and the Creation of Community.* Masters Thesis at the University of New Orleans.

Cruz, Jan Cohen. 2005. *Local Acs: Community-Based Performance in the United States.* Piscataway, New Jersey: Rutgers University Press.

Diamond, Stanley. 2017 (orig. 1974). *In Search of the Primitive: A Critique of Civilization.* New York: Routeledge.

— 1960. *Culture in History: Essays in Honor of Paul Radin.* New York: Columbia University Press.

Drewal, Henry John and John Mason. 1997. *Beads, Body, and Soul: Art and Light in the Yoruba Universe.* Los Angeles: UCLA Fowler Museum of Cultural History.

Drewal, Margaret Thompson. 1992. *Yoruba Ritual: Performers, Play, Agency.* Bloomington: Indiana University Press.

Drewal, Henry John and Margaret Thompson Drewal. 1990. *Gelede: Art and Female Power Among the Yoruba.* Bloomington: Indiana University Press.

Ehrenreich, Jeffrey David. 2004. "Bodies, Beads, Bones and Feathers: The Masking Tradition of Mardi Gras Indians in New Orleans, A Photo Essay." *City & Society* 16 (1): 117–150.

— 2010. "Drumming, African Identity, and Shamanism: The SSC and the Ritual State of the Spirit of Fi Yi Yi in the Black (Mardi Gras) Indian Tradition of New Orleans." *Shamanism Annual.* Vol. 23: 5–11.

Evans, Freddi Williams. 2011. *Congo Square: African Roots in New Orleans*. Lafayette, LA: University of Louisiana at Lafayette.

Faris, James. 2003. "Navajo and Photography." *Photography's Other Histories*, edited by Christopher Pinney and Nicolas Peterson. Durham: Duke University Press: 85-99.

Freire, Paulo. 2000 (orig. 1969). *Pedagogy of the Oppressed*. London: Bloomsbury Academic.

Gordon, Deborah A. 1995. "Border Work: Feminist Ethnography and the Dissemination of Literacy" and "Conclusion: Culture Writing Women: Inscribing Feminist Anthropology" in *Women Writing Culture*. Edited by Ruth Behar and Deborah A. Gordon. Berkeley: University of California Press. 373–389, 429–441.

Glaze, Anita J. 1986. "Dialectics of Gender in Senufo Masquerades." *African Arts* 19 (3): 30–39; 82.

Harner, Michael. 1980. *The Way of the Shaman*. New York: Harper and Row.

Haviland, Maya. 2017. *Side by Side? Community-Based Art and the Challenge of Co-Creativity*. New York: Routledge.

Katzman, Lisa. 2005. *Tootie's Last Suit*. Video. New York: Pomegranate Productions.

Lee, Dorothy. 1987 (orig. 1959). *Freedom and Culture*. Prospect Heights, IL: Waveland Press.

— 1986. *Valuing the Self: What We Can Learn from Other Cultures*. Long Grove, IL: Waveland Press.

McCarthy Brown, Karen. 1992. *Mama Lola: A Vodou Priestess in Brooklyn*. Berkeley: University of California Press.

Myerhoff, Barbara. 1978. *Number Our Days*. New York: Touchstone Books.

Nunley, John W. and Cara McCarty. 1999. *Masks: Faces of Culture*. New York: Abrams.

Nunley, John W. and Judith Bettelheim. 1988. *Caribbean Festival Arts: Each and Every Bit of Difference*. Seattle: University of Washington Press.

Radin, Paul. 1963. *The Autobiography of a Winnebago Indian*. New York: Dover Publications, Inc.

Reed, Ishmael. 1972. "The Neo-HooDoo Manifesto." *Conjure*. Amherst: University of Massachusetts Press.

Regis, Helen A., Rachel Breunlin, and Ronald W. Lewis. 2010. "Building Collaborative Partnerships Through a Lower Ninth Ward Museum." *Practicing Anthropology* 33 (2): 4–10.

Regis, Helen. 2001. "Blackness and the Politics of Memory in the New Orleans Second Line." *American Ethnologist* 28 (4): 752–777.

— 1999. "Second lines, Minstresy, and the Contested Landscape of New Orleans' Afro-Creole Festivals." *Cultural Anthropology*. 14 (4): 472–504.

Roberts, Mary Nooter and Allen Nooter, eds. 1996. *Memory: Luba Art and the Making of History*. New York: Prestel Verlag.

Schjeldahl, Peter. 2008. "Come On Down: The New Orleans Biennial Beckons." *The New Yorker*. November 28: 128–129.

Smith, Michael P. 1994. *Mardi Gras Indians*. New Orleans: Pelican Publishing.

— 1987. *Spirit World: Pattern in the Expressive Folk Culture of Afro-American New Orleans*. New Orleans: New Orleans Urban Folk Society.

Smith, Roberta. 2008. "Kaleidescope Biennial for a Scarred City." *The New York Times*. November 4, C1.

Tancons, Claire and Krista Thompson, eds. 2016. *EN MAS': Carnival and Performance Art in the Caribbean*. New Orleans: Independent Curators International and the Contemporary Art Center.

Tancons, Claire. 2008. "The Greatest Free Show On Earth: Carnival from Trinidad to Brazil, Cape Town to New Orleans." *Prospect.1 New Orleans*. Brooklyn, NY: PictureBox. 42–53.

Thompson, Robert Ferris. 2005. "When Saints Go Marching In: Kongo Louisiana, Kongo New Orleans." *Resonance from the Past: African Sculpture from the New Orleans Museum of Art*. Edited by Frank Herreman. New York: Museum for African Art, New York: 136–143.

— 1984. *Flash of the Spirit: African and Afro-American Art and Philosophy*. New York: Vintage Books.

— 1970. "The Sign of the Divine King: An Essay on Yoruba Bead-Embroidered Crowns with Veil and Bird Decorations." *African Arts* 3 (3): 8–17, 74–80.

Walker, Aaron. 2010. *Bury the Hatchet*. Video. New Orleans: Ciné Marais and Altaire Productions.

Wyckoff, Geraldine. 2014. "Sudan Social and Pleasure Club Dances for Peace." *Offbeat Magazine*: http://www.offbeat.com/articles/sudan-social-aid-pleasure-club-dances-peace. Last accessed November 12, 2017.